World Book's

SCIENCE
& NATURE
GUIDES

SEA SHELLS

OF THE UNITED STATES AND CANADA

World Book, Inc.
a Scott Fetzer company
Chicago

Scientific names

In this book, after the common name of an organism (life form) is given, that organism's scientific name usually appears. Scientific names are put into a special type of lettering, called italic, *which looks like this.*

The first name in a scientific name is the genus. A genus consists of very similar groups, but the members of these different groups usually cannot breed with one another. The second name given is the species. Every known organism belongs to a particular species. Members of a species can breed with one another, and the young grow up to look very much like the parents.

An animal's scientific name is the same worldwide. This helps scientists and students to know which animal is being discussed, since the animal may have many different common names.

Therefore, when you see a name like *Siliqua costata,* you know that the genus is *Siliqua* and the species is *costata* for the Atlantic razor (see page 16).

Shell-collector's Code

Beaches can be dangerous places.

1 **Keep a careful eye on the tide,** and make sure you can reach safety if the tide begins to come in.

2 **Always go collecting with a friend,** and always tell an adult where you are going.

3 **Don't walk beneath overhanging cliffs.**

4 **Avoid doing any damage to the environment** or harming any living creature you may come across.

5 **Take your litter home with you.**

6 **Ask permission** before crossing private property to reach a beach or before going on a private wharf.

This edition published in the United States of America by World Book, Inc., Chicago.

WORLD BOOK and the GLOBE DEVICE are registered trademarks or trademarks of World Book, Inc.

World Book, Inc.
233 North Michigan Avenue
Chicago, IL 60601 USA

For information about other World Book publications, visit our Web site **http://www.worldbook.com** or call **1-800-WORLDBK (967-5325).** For information about sales to schools and libraries, call **1-800-975-3250 (United States); 1-800-837-5365 (Canada).**

Copyright © 2007, 2005 Anova Books Company Ltd.
151 Freston Road, London W10 6TH, United Kingdom
www.anovabooks.com

The Library of Congress has cataloged an earlier edition of this title as follows:

Sea shells of the United States and Canada.
    p. cm. — (World Book's science & nature guides)
    Includes bibliographical references and index.
    ISBN 0-7166-4218-2 — ISBN 0-7166-4208-5 (set)
    1. Shells--United States--Identification. 2. Shells--Canada--Identification. I. Series.
QL414 .S42 2005
594.147'7'097—dc22

                                    2004043489

This edition: ISBN 13: 978-0-7166-4230-5   ISBN 10: 0-7166-4230-1
ISBN 13 (set): 978-0-7166-4221-3   ISBN 10 (set): 0-7166-4221-2

The author and publishers would like to thank Dr. R. Tucker Abbott for lending the majority of the photographs illustrating this book.
© R. Tucker Abbott, 1994
© David Parmiter, 1994; pages 8–9, 58–59
The Academy of Natural Sciences; page 26 (bottom, right), page 27 (top, right), page 39 (bottom, left), page 46 (bottom, left)
Activity illustrations by Richard Coombes;
headbands by Antonia Phillips.

For World Book:
Editor-in-Chief: Paul A. Kobasa
Editorial: Shawn Brennan, Lisa Kwon, Maureen Liebenson, Christine Sullivan
Research: Mike Barr, Madolynn Cronk, Lynn Durbin, Cheryl Graham, Jacqueline Jasek, Karen McCormack, and Loranne Shields
Librarian: Stephanie Kitchen
Permissions: Janet Peterson
Graphics and Design: Sandra Dyrlund, Isaiah Sheppard
Indexing: Aamir Burki, David Pofelski
Pre-press and Manufacturing: Carma Fazio, Anne Fritzinger, Steven Hueppchen, Madelyn Underwood
Text Processing: Curley Hunter, Gwendolyn Johnson
Proofreading: Anne Dillon

Printed in China
2 3 4 5 6 7 8 9 10 09 08 07 06

Contents

Entries *like this* indicate pages featuring projects you can do!

Introduction To Shells

Sea shells are all over the Atlantic and Pacific beaches of the United States and Canada. These hard, usually colorful cases once provided homes for living animals—animals related to the snails that you may find in your yard, for instance. They belong to a group called the mollusks.

You can learn a lot about mollusks and their life by collecting their shells and also by studying live specimens in temporary aquariums. This book will show you how to collect them, and it explains the different kinds of mollusks. Sea shells come from mollusks that live in the ocean. There are about 100,000 different mollusks worldwide, but when looking for sea shells, you are unlikely to find more than a few hundred, even if you search every beach in North America! This book shows you some of the most common shells you may encounter.

Some mollusks live in warm water, others in colder water. This book divides the seas around the U.S. and Canada into four areas, according to the average sea temperature. Some species can be found in more than one area, because they can tolerate a wide range of temperatures or have adapted to local conditions. A species is listed under the geographic area in which it is most likely found.

Mollusks lay masses of eggs, so at least a few will hatch and survive

As the mollusk grows, its shell grows with it. When the mollusk is fully formed, it will be ready to produce more eggs

The egg hatches into a larva

The larva begins to grow a shell. Its oarlike flaps are covered with tiny hairs, which help it to swim until it finds a rock or other place to settle

Life cycle

Different species of mollusks reproduce in different ways. Some mollusks are hermaphrodites. That is, one animal is both male and female. In hermaphroditic species, the mollusk lays its eggs and then self-fertilizes those eggs. Some species of mollusks have separate males and females (as humans do).

Northern Atlantic coast: Newfoundland and Labrador to Virginia. Temperature about 52 °F (11 °C).
Southern Atlantic coast: North Carolina to Texas. Temperature about 85 °F (29 °C).
Northern Pacific coast: Alaska to Central California. Temperature about 52 °F (11 °C).
Southern Pacific coast: Southern California. Temperature about 75 °F (24 °C).

(All temperatures are ranges at the water's surface. F = Fahrenheit; C = Celsius.)

How to use this book

To identify a shell you don't recognize—for example, the two shown at left—follow these steps.

1. **Find the section of this book** that describes your area.
2. **Decide what kind of beach you are on.** Does it have rocky pools or sand or mud flats? Is it an estuary? Each habitat (type of beach) has a different picture band (see below).
3. **Decide what sort of mollusk you have found.** Is it a gastropod or a bivalve? See pages 6 and 7 if you don't know the difference.
4. **Look through the pages of shells** for the type you have found. The information and photo given for each mollusk will help you to identify it. You will find the gastropod shell on page 11—it's a rough periwinkle.
5. **If you can't find the shell,** look through the pages concerning other kinds of shore. A shell from a sandy beach might have been carried by the tide to a rocky one. You will find the bivalve shell on page 13; it's a blue mussel.
6. **If you still can't find the shell,** try looking in sections in this book covering neighboring areas, or in a larger field guide. NOTE: Some photos are enlarged to show detail. Lengths supplied in boldface type are average lengths.

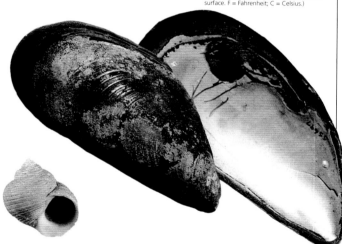

Top-of-page Picture Bands

Each habitat (type of beach) has a different picture band at the top of the page. These are shown below.

 **Estuaries and Salt Marshes**

 **Sand and Mud Flats**

Rocky Shores and Pools

Wood and Rock (Borers)

You will find two or three of these habitats in each of the four sections of this book.

What To Look For

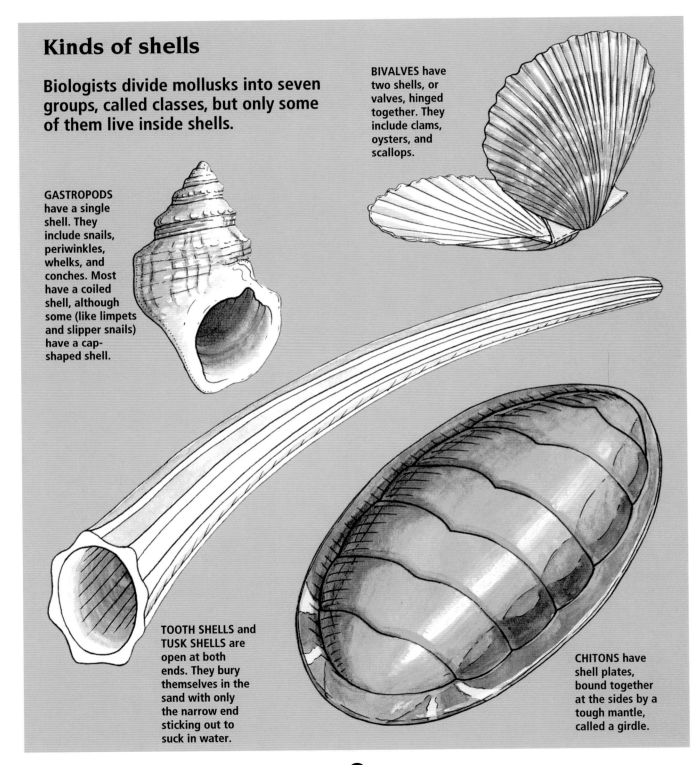

Kinds of shells

Biologists divide mollusks into seven groups, called classes, but only some of them live inside shells.

BIVALVES have two shells, or valves, hinged together. They include clams, oysters, and scallops.

GASTROPODS have a single shell. They include snails, periwinkles, whelks, and conches. Most have a coiled shell, although some (like limpets and slipper snails) have a cap-shaped shell.

TOOTH SHELLS and TUSK SHELLS are open at both ends. They bury themselves in the sand with only the narrow end sticking out to suck in water.

CHITONS have shell plates, bound together at the sides by a tough mantle, called a girdle.

Parts of a shell

This is a gastropod shell. Most gastropod shells are right handed—that is, when looking down from the apex, the shell winds in a clockwise direction.

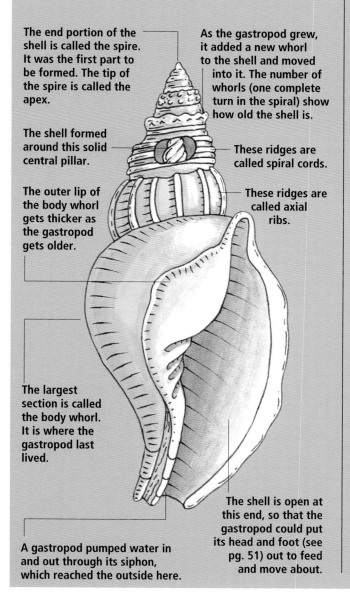

The end portion of the shell is called the spire. It was the first part to be formed. The tip of the spire is called the apex.

As the gastropod grew, it added a new whorl to the shell and moved into it. The number of whorls (one complete turn in the spiral) show how old the shell is.

The shell formed around this solid central pillar.

These ridges are called spiral cords.

The outer lip of the body whorl gets thicker as the gastropod gets older.

These ridges are called axial ribs.

The largest section is called the body whorl. It is where the gastropod last lived.

The shell is open at this end, so that the gastropod could put its head and foot (see pg. 51) out to feed and move about.

A gastropod pumped water in and out through its siphon, which reached the outside here.

This is one half of a bivalve shell. The shape of the scars (where a muscle was once attached) and the number of hinge teeth help to identify bivalves.

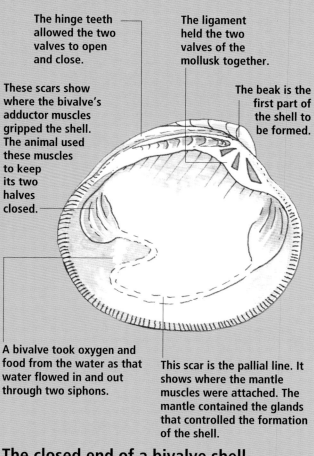

The hinge teeth allowed the two valves to open and close.

The ligament held the two valves of the mollusk together.

These scars show where the bivalve's adductor muscles gripped the shell. The animal used these muscles to keep its two halves closed.

The beak is the first part of the shell to be formed.

A bivalve took oxygen and food from the water as that water flowed in and out through two siphons.

This scar is the pallial line. It shows where the mantle muscles were attached. The mantle contained the glands that controlled the formation of the shell.

The closed end of a bivalve shell

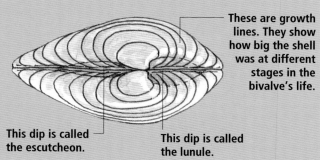

These are growth lines. They show how big the shell was at different stages in the bivalve's life.

This dip is called the escutcheon.

This dip is called the lunule.

Atlantic Coast: Newfoundland and Labrador to Virginia

The section of Atlantic coastline that runs from Newfoundland and Labrador to Virginia is fairly rich in mollusk species that live in shallow-water and shore areas. There is an enormous variation in the types of shore, from the extensive, intertidal mud flats of the Bay of Fundy to the rocky coasts of Nova Scotia, and to the sandy beaches of Cape Cod.

Malacologists (zoologists who study mollusks) divide this region into two provinces. The stretch from Newfoundland and Labrador to Cape Cod is called the Acadian province, and from Cape Cod to Cape Hatteras is called the Virginian province.

New England has hundreds of species of mollusks, but most of them are in offshore waters and are not often found on the beach. Sometimes, however, specimens are found washed up after storms or abandoned by the receding tides.

Rock pools further away from the ocean are generally less likely to have shells in them. If it is sunny for a long time, some of the water in such a pool may evaporate and the remainder will become too salty for the mollusks. If there is a drenching rainstorm, it may dilute the seawater and cause the pool to be too fresh. Mollusks like conditions to be just right, so not as many varieties have adapted to live in the changeable environment of a rock pool.

Rocky Shores & Pools

of Newfoundland and Labrador to Virginia

At high tide, rocky shores can have waves so rough that they wash most living organisms away. But at low tide you may find limpets and periwinkles clinging to rocks, sometimes under hanging seaweed. There is no better protected area for some types of mollusks and other sea creatures than the pools of clear seawater that are left by the receding tide, where there are no rough waves to contend with.

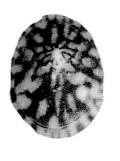 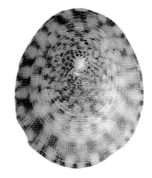 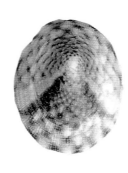

Atlantic Plate Limpet
(Tectura testudinalis)

All limpets live on rocks. Each limpet's shell grows to fit the patch of rock where it lives, so that when a limpet attaches to a rock not even the strongest wave can dislodge it. This species of limpet can be found clinging to rocks from the Arctic coasts to Long Island, New York. It has an oval shell with the apex (end point) of its dome nearly in the center. The outside of the shell is a dull cream-gray with bars and streaks of brown. Inside it is a bluish-white with a brown center.
Limpet family
About 1 in (2.5 cm) long

Atlantic Dogwinkle
(Nucella lapillus)

This spindle-shaped shell has a tall spire. The shell may be smooth or have spiral threads. It is usually a dull white, but it may be yellowish and have dark brown spiral bands. This winkle feeds on barnacles and small mussels; it lays its eggs encased in leathery capsules. The winkle gives off a purple dye, which was once used for marking laundry. The shell is found from southern Labrador to New York.
Dogwinkle family—About 1 in (2.5 cm) long

Common Periwinkle
(Littorina littorea)

Periwinkles are a type of snail. This species is one of the largest periwinkles. It is common on intertidal rocks from northern Canada to Delaware. It has a solid, globular shell with a strong, thin outer lip. The color is a drab gray, sometimes with fine, white streaks in a spiral pattern. Like all periwinkles, this snail is an herbivore.
Periwinkle family
Up to 1½ in (4 cm) long

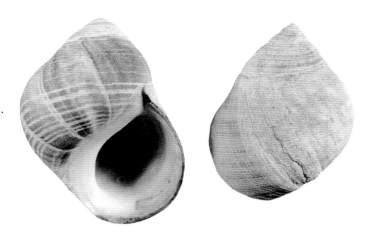

Yellow Periwinkle
(Littorina obtusata)

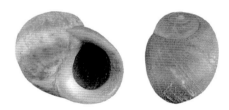

The solid, ball-shaped shell of this small periwinkle is usually a bright, brownish-yellow, and it may have a brown or white spiral band. This species of periwinkle is flatter than many others. These snails tend to hide under clumps of overhanging seaweeds, on which the female lays her jellylike egg masses. This periwinkle is common from southern Labrador to New Jersey.
Periwinkle family
About ½ in (1 cm) long

Rough Periwinkle
(Littorina saxatilis)

This periwinkle also has a solid shell, but is much more pointed in shape than the yellow periwinkle. The surface of the shell has spiral cords and fine threads, and the color is gray with a darker pattern and a dark aperture (main opening of the shell). This periwinkle is common from the Arctic seas to New Jersey. The females give birth to live young complete with shells.
Periwinkle family
About ½ in (1 cm) long

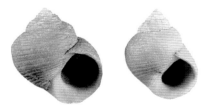

Prickly Jingle
(Anomia squamula)

Be careful when touching this little shell—the curved upper valve is often covered with small spines. The shell is very thin. The lower shell is flat and has a small hole near the hinge. The mollusk pushes its strong byssus (see glossary) through this opening and uses it to attach itself to a rock. These shells are found from Labrador to North Carolina.
Jingle shell family
About ¾ in (2 cm) long

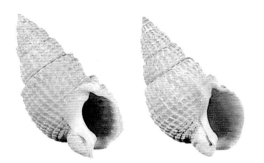

Threeline Mud Snail
(Nassarius trivittatus)

This sea snail lives below the low tidemark (see pg. 22), usually on clear sand, and eats dead fish and shrimp. The threeline mud snail (also called New England nassa) is common from Newfoundland to northern Florida. It has a knobby, pointed spiral shell with eight or nine stepped whorls. The aperture has a sharp outer lip.
Nassa mud snail family
About ¾ in (2 cm) long

Eastern White Slipper Snail
(Crepidula plana)

This sea snail has a thin, white shell. The shell may be concave or convex, depending on what it is attached to. These snails group together on or inside empty shells left by dead animals. Males stack on top of female partners. If the female of this group dies, a male turns into a female. This snail is very common from Canada to Texas.
Slipper snail family
About 1¼ in (3 cm) long

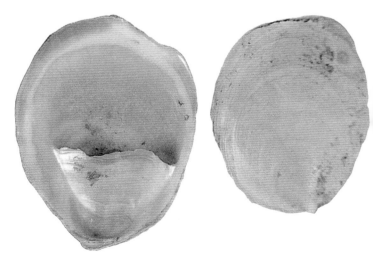

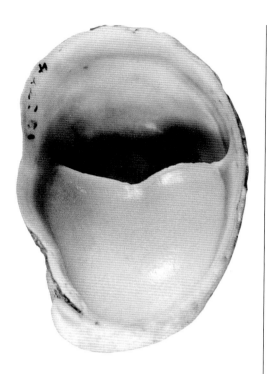

Common Atlantic Slipper Snail
(Crepidula fornicata)

Slipper snails get their name from their peculiar shape, which is like a slipper or shoe. An overhang, or deck, of shell extends over the rear half of the inside of this shell. The outside of the shell ranges in color from dirty-white to tan. Individuals usually stack on top of one another, with the female underneath and the male on top. This shell is common from the maritime provinces of Canada to Texas.
Slipper snail family
About 1½ in (4 cm) long

Blue Mussel
(Mytilus edulis)

The blue mussel gets its name from its deep blue-black outer shell. The inner shell of this bivalve is a pearly-white with a deep blue border. This mussel is found in large colonies attached to intertidal rocks all down the eastern seaboard to South Carolina. At low tide it shuts its valves firmly to keep moisture in.
Mussel family
Up to 3 in (7.5 cm) long

Sand & Mud Flats

of Newfoundland and Labrador to Virginia

Sand and mud flats (nearly level tidal areas) provide homes for many species of mollusks. These areas are uncovered only at low tide. Don't confuse them with sandy beaches that slope into the water. Look for mollusks by following their trails in the sand, or by digging below clam holes.

A snail that lives in these habitats will use its large foot to creep across the sand. Many snails feed on fragments of edible material—both animal and vegetable—that are found on the surface. Some bivalves burrow into the sand or mud, leaving just their feeding siphons projecting. Many of these bivalves are filter feeders, drawing in water and filtering out edible particles from it.

Bay Scallop
(Argopecten irradians)

This is a common edible scallop, found at depths of 3-65 feet (1-20 meters) from the northern shore of Cape Cod south to New Jersey. It has a solid, almost circular shell with 17 or 18 low, rounded ribs. The color is usually a drab gray-brown, mottled with dark brown. The lower valve is slightly lighter in color than the upper one. The ears of the valves are of almost equal size. This species is the state shell of New York.

Scallop family
About 3 in
(7.5 cm) long

Atlantic Nut Clam
(Nucula proxima)

This tiny, hard-shelled clam is common in sand and mud from Nova Scotia to Texas. It has a solid shell, greenish gray with irregular, brownish rings. The outer shell has an oily shine. The inside of the shell is pearly. The hinge has many small teeth.
Nut clam family
About 1/4 in (0.5 cm) long

Bruised Nassa
(Nassarius vibex)

Mud flats from Cape Cod and south to Texas are the home of this common little mud snail. It has a solid, ribbed shell, colored gray-brown to whitish with darker brown blotches. The outer lip of the aperture (main opening) has four or five enamel teeth. It is also known as the common eastern nassa.
Nassa mud snail family
About ½ in (1 cm) long

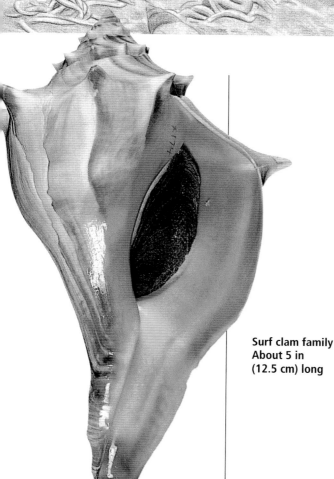

Atlantic Surf Clam
(Spisula solidissima)

This is a very common, edible species of clam that lives in shallow water. It is fished commercially (by dredging—pulling a large net behind a boat to scrape the sea bottom). This clam has a smooth shell, almost oval in shape, with a sunken pit in the center of the hinge.

Surf clam family
About 5 in
(12.5 cm) long

Knobbed Whelk
(Busycon carica)

This huge snail is a meat-eater that feeds on clams; most members of its family live in tropical waters. This common whelk lives in the shallow waters of the intertidal flats from Cape Cod into the southern United States. It is named for the spines, or knobs, on its shell. This species is the state shell for Georgia and New Jersey.
Busycon whelk family
About 7 in (18 cm) long

Northern Moon Snail
(Euspira heros)

Animals of this species are much larger than the spotted species of snails. Moon snails have a globular shell colored brownish-gray to dirty-white. The aperture is glossy and tan-colored or marked with purplish-brown stains. The female lays an egg case that is a wide, open dome of sand with the tiny eggs embedded in it. The case crumbles when dry.
Moon snail family
About 4 in (10 cm) long

Sand & Mud Flats

of Newfoundland and Labrador to Virginia

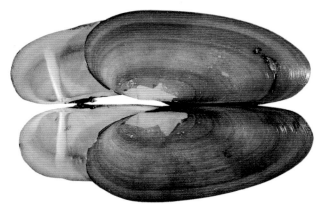

Atlantic Razor
(Siliqua costata)

Unlike most other razors, this clam is shaped in an elongated oval. The shell is thin and delicate, and the overlayer of the shell has a greenish tinge. The inside of the shell is a glossy purplish-white with a strong white rib. This clam burrows into firm sand and is a common species found from the Gulf of St. Lawrence to North Carolina.
Razor clam family
About 2 in (5 cm) long

Sandy Lyonsia
(Lyonsia arenosa)

The tiny sandy lyonsia is named for the dusting of sand grains cemented to the overlayer of its shell. It belongs to a family of fragile clams that are usually distorted in shape because they nestle in rock crevices, sponges, and peat. The shell is almost oblong. This species is fairly common from Greenland to New England.
Lyonsia family
About ½ in (1 cm) long

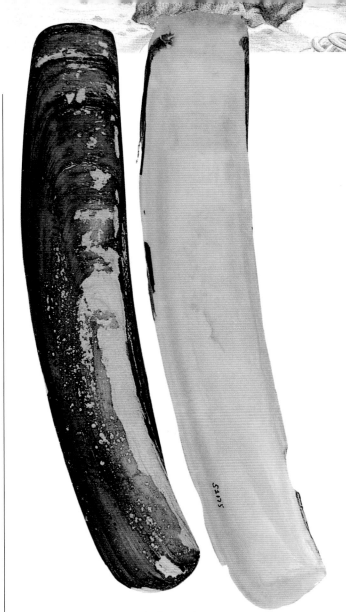

Atlantic Jackknife
(Ensis directus)

This very long clam looks like an old-fashioned straight-edge razor. The clam has a smooth shell, with the two valves forming a slightly curved cylinder. There are wide gapes (holes) at each end. The shell is basically white, with a varnishlike overlayer of brownish-green. It is a common edible species that lives in sand burrows from southern Labrador to South Carolina.
Razor clam family
About 9 in (23 cm) long

Chalky Macoma
(Macoma calcarea)

The chalky macoma belongs to a family of bivalves known as tellins. Its shell is an elongated oval, with a gray overlayer, which is usually worn away except at the edges. The beak is not central but is instead about three-fifths of the way across the back end. This is a common cold-water species, found offshore from Greenland to New York.
Tellin family—About 2 in (5 cm) long

Variable Coquina
(Donax variabilis)

The coquina is a tiny clam with a wedge-shaped shell. From Maryland northward the shell color is dull white with purple rays. In warmer waters farther south the color varies considerably, but it is usually bright. The coquina is found from New York to Texas. Unlike most clams, wedge clams live in a habitat along wave-dashed, sandy beaches, where they are found in large colonies.
Wedge clam family
About ½ in (1 cm) long

Softshell Clam
(Mya arenaria)

This is an edible clam, commonly found in mud flats or sandy flats along the Atlantic shore as far south as South Carolina. It has a smooth, thin shell. This shell gapes open at the rear end where, in live specimens, the siphon projects. People dig for these clams at low tide. Other names for this mollusk are the gaper clam, steamer clam, and long-necked clam.
Softshell clam family—About 4 in (10 cm) long

Gould Pandora
(Pandora gouldiana)

This is a small, flat, cold-water clam. Its thick shell is compressed and is shaped like a half-moon. In most specimens the white and chalky shell is partly worn away and shows the pearly underlayers. It is found from the Gulf of St. Lawrence to North Carolina, in the intertidal zone (see pg. 22) and deeper.
Pandora clam family
About 1 in (2.5 cm) long

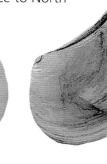

Estuaries & Salt Marshes

of Newfoundland and Labrador to Virginia

An estuary is where a river meets with a sea or ocean. The waters of estuaries are brackish—that is, they contain a mixture of salt water from the sea and fresh water from the river. Brackish water is also found in salt marshes—muddy areas that blend into the sea. Only certain species of mussels and clams do well in brackish water, and some types of oysters also enjoy this habitat. Wading birds, ducks, and crabs feed on estuary mollusks. In the salt marshes, tall grasses and reeds offer protection to many kinds of mollusks. Mollusks, in these habitats, however, must endure changing tides, water levels, and salt levels.

Pointed Cingula
(Onoba aculeus)

The pointed cingula belongs to a family of extremely small snails—so tiny that a teaspoon will hold dozens of them. It is one of many different species that are so similar, only experts can tell them apart. The pointed cingula specimens shown here give an idea of how small these snails can be. This species lives among seaweed in shallow, brackish water from Nova Scotia to New Jersey.
Rissoid family—About ⅛ in (0.3 cm) long

Solitary Glassy-bubble
(Haminoea solitaria)

This small snail belongs to a group whose members are hermaphrodites—that is, each snail has both male and female sex organs. It has a fragile shell, with the aperture extending the entire length of the shell. The shell's color varies from translucent amber to whitish. This snail prefers a shallow, sandy area where it can hide among grasses; it lays its eggs on weed stems. The range of this mollusk is from Cape Cod to North Carolina.
**Bubble shell family
About ½ in (1 cm) long**

Thick-lip Drill
(Eupleura caudata)

This is another common species that lives by using a filelike tongue and chemicals that its body produces to make a hole in the shells of young oysters. It then feeds off the soft body of the oyster. The thick-lip drill has a more rugged-looking shell than that of the Atlantic oyster drill. The outer lip of the body whorl of the thick-lip drill is thick, with raised teeth. It is found from south of Cape Cod to southern Florida. Although similar in form to the Atlantic oyster drill, these two mollusks are not closely related.
**Murex family
About 1 in (2.5 cm) long**

Atlantic Oyster Drill

(Urosalpinx cinerea)

This little snail is the worst enemy of oysters. It "drills" a hole in an oyster's shell. It then eats the oyster's soft body. The Atlantic oyster drill can destroy much of the crop in some commercial oyster beds. It is a dirty-gray or yellow in color with a brown aperture. Its range is from Nova Scotia to northeastern Florida.
Murex family
About 1 in (2.5 cm) long

Baltic Macoma

(Macoma balthica)

The Baltic macoma is a bivalve of the tellin family. It has a fairly small, oval-shaped shell that is moderately compressed. The shell is dull white in color, sometimes tinged with pink. The overlayer is thin and gray and tends to flake off when dry. The Baltic macoma is a very common intertidal and offshore species found from Greenland to Georgia.
Tellin family—About 1 in (2.5 cm) long

Dark False Mussel

(Mytilopsis leucophaeata)

This small, common bivalve belongs to a family of clams that have taken on the shape and habits of some mussels. This false mussel is found in brackish to fresh waters near rivers from New York to Texas. It attaches itself to rocks and twigs, in clumps that look like colonies of mussels. The overlayer of the shell is thin and somewhat glossy. It is also known as Conrad false mussel.
False mussel family—About ¾ in (2 cm) long

Eastern Oyster

(Crassostrea virginica)

The eastern oyster is a large bivalve, with slightly wavy edges to its shells. The lower valve is cup-shaped with a deep purple mark where the muscle was attached. The shape varies. This oyster ranges from Cape Cod to Texas, and can also be found locally north to Maine and in the Gulf of St. Lawrence. The shell of this species is the state shell for Mississippi, Virginia, and Connecticut.
Oyster family—About 5 in (12.5 cm) long

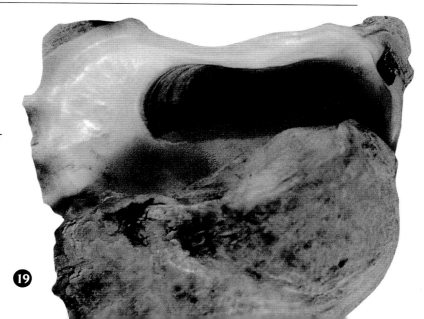

Northern Quahog
(Mercenaria mercenaria)

This is a large clam that is almost as popular a seafood as the oyster. It is common in shallow, brackish water from Quebec to Texas. It is a bulky bivalve; the shell is gray with fine growth lines. The inside is white with purple stains. The Pequot Indian word quahog (pronounced KWOH hawg) means "hard clam." American Indians formerly used these shells as money. The quahog is also called a hard-shell or cherrystone clam. This species provides the state shell for Rhode Island.
Venus clam family
About 4 in (10 cm) long

False Quahog
(Pitar morrhuanus)

The small false quahog is also used as food—but by bottom-living fish, not humans. The exterior of the somewhat bulky shell is dull gray to brownish-red with fine growth lines. It is found in shallow water from the Gulf of St. Lawrence south to North Carolina. It is also called the morrhua venus.
Venus clam family
About 1 in (2.5 cm) long

Amethyst Gem Clam
(Gemma gemma)

Dozens of these tiny clams can fit into a teaspoon. They live under the sand in shallow water from Nova Scotia south to Texas. Sea birds and small fish eat large quantities of them. The outside of the thin shell is whitish-tan or purple in color, and it is covered with many thin ribs.
Venus clam family
About ⅛ in (0.3 cm) long

There are many salt marshes close to the sea where the water is brackish. Meadows of tall grasses and reeds offer protection to several special kinds of mollusks, but the animals have to be able to endure changing water levels caused by the tides, temperature extremes, and wide ranges in salt content.

Eastern Melampus
(Melampus bidentatus)

This small snail breathes air with a lung, as does the familiar garden snail, instead of removing oxygen from the water with gills. It is very common in salt marshes from eastern Quebec to Texas. It lives on grass stems, where it lays its jellylike egg masses. The snail is a hermaphrodite (it has both male and female sex parts) and is an herbivore. The shells are smooth, shining brown when fresh, sometimes featuring three or four darker bands.
Marsh snail family
About ½ in (1 cm) long

Marsh Periwinkle
(Littoraria irrorata)

This periwinkle lives in large numbers among the sedges (tufted plants) of brackish marshes. It has a thick shell with many spiral grooves. It is grayish in color with short streaks of reddish-brown on the spiral ridges. The aperture is red. It is found from New York to Texas.
Periwinkle family
About 1 in (2.5 cm) long

Eastern Mud Snail
(Nassarius obsoletus)

This is a very common species on intertidal mud flats. It has a solid, smoothish shell with a high spire. The color of the shell is dark brown with a narrow, tan band on the middle of the last whorl. The aperture is chocolate-brown and is one-third the length of the shell. This snail is found from Quebec to northeastern Florida.
Nassa mud snail family
About ¾ in (2 cm) long

Ribbed Mussel
(Geukensia demissa)

This large, strong, but lightweight mussel is very common in intertidal grass and peat marshlands. Its range is from the Gulf of St. Lawrence to northeastern Florida. The long shell is typically black and brown on the outside with strong, rough radial ribs. The whitish inside has darker coloring at the wide end.
Mussel family
About 3 in (7.5 cm) long

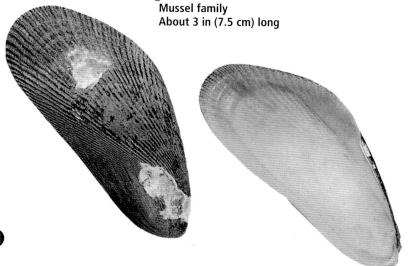

Explore the Shore

The types of shells you find depend on what kind of beach you explore. The best beaches to search are sandy and muddy ones for burrowing mollusks, or rocky beaches for the mollusks that hide in crevices, cling to rocks, or are stranded in rock pools.

You will not find many shells on a shingle (pebble) beach, because the sea moves the stones about, smashing empty shells and making life impossible for living mollusks. At low tide the shingle dries out, which again is not a good habitat for sea snails and bivalves.

Beach zones

You can divide every beach into five zones (shown below). They are governed by the rise and fall of the tide. High tide occurs about every 12 hours 25 minutes, and low tide is about 6 hours 13 minutes after high tide. You can find out from tide tables when the next low tide is due.

Roughly twice a month there are higher tides than usual. These are called **spring** tides, although they have nothing to do with the season of spring. In between the spring tides there are lower tides than usual, called **neap** tides. The shore between the highest point covered by spring tides and the lowest point uncovered by neap tides is the **intertidal** zone, and it is there that you will do most of your exploring.

Make a beach map

If you are on the beach around low tide, why not make a map of the tidal zones? All you need is a long piece of string, a tape measure, a notebook, and a pencil.

1 **Tie one end of the string** to a rock or piece of driftwood and put it just above the line of debris washed up by the ocean, which marks the edge of the splash zone.
2 **Tie the other end** to a rock or stick and place it at the edge of the water.

The SPLASH ZONE is wetted by spray at high tide, but is covered only when storms drive waves on to the beach.

The UPPER ZONE is often uncovered, even at high tide.

The MIDDLE ZONE is the largest area. It is always uncovered at low tide.

The LOWER ZONE is uncovered only during neap tides.

The SHALLOW-WATER ZONE is always covered by water, even at low tide.

COCKLE BAY - 3rd June   LOW TIDE

3 yards Splash zone	Periwinkles	Brown seaweed
7 yards Upper zone	razorshell	Green seaweed
15 yards middle zone	oil	old rope	crab claw
10 yards Lower zone	mussels		cockle

3 **Use pebbles or driftwood** to show where the different zones start.
4 **Measure each zone with the tape measure** and record that distance.
5 **Make a list of what you find in each zone**— shells, seaweed, rubbish that is a form of pollution (see right), and anything else of interest. Is there a band of pebbles or an outcrop of rocks?
6 **When you go to another beach** and do this survey again, compare the two maps to see how the beaches differ.

Pollution survey

Patrolling a beach and making a list of what is on it that shouldn't be is a good activity for you and some friends. Try to work out for yourself where the various kinds of pollution have come from. These are some of the things to look out for:
1 **Glass:** mostly bottles and often broken.
2 **Plastic and polyethylene:** some plastics eventually break down, but polyethylene doesn't.
3 **Wood.**
4 **Canisters and barrels:** these often still have their contents, which can range from chemicals to food. They don't always have a label to tell you what is inside. **Don't touch these,** but report them to the nearest Coast Guard or the police as soon as possible. **They may be dangerous.**
5 **Oil:** usually appears as patches of black tar, which can be very difficult to remove from your clothes. Use olive oil on a pad of cotton to clean up.
6 **Dead fish and sea birds:** do not touch or handle any dead bird or fish. If, however, you find a dead animal that has a band around its leg, contact a wildlife organization.
7 **Wire, plain or barbed.**
8 **Bits of metal,** such as sheets of corrugated iron.
9 **Sewage:** this includes anything that goes down your toilet, in addition to disposable diapers. **Do not touch these items.** And, touch nothing that seems medical in nature, such as a hypodermic needle.

Pollution on our beaches is a major problem. Some pollution is made up of trash discarded by thoughtless people using the beaches, but a lot of trash originates from ships and is then washed ashore. In some areas, beach pollution is caused by sewage that has been pumped out to sea, but which is then washed back to the shore by the tide.

Atlantic Coast: North Carolina to Texas

This stretch of the North Atlantic coast is washed by warmer waters than the northern part, and so it is home to many more species. In the southern part there are a number of tropical species, as well.

Most of the waters from North Carolina to Texas have cooler water with low, flat shorelines, where extensive stretches of estuaries, tidal flats, and low salt marshes support many shallow-water mollusks. This is known as the Carolinian province.

The long peninsula of Florida makes a break in this province. Its southern tip and the string of islands along the lower Florida Keys are bathed by the warm waters of the Gulf Stream and Caribbean Sea. That is why this area has many tropical species of sea shells also found in the Caribbean and is part of the Caribbean province.

The climate in the Carolinian and Caribbean provinces varies from cool winters to hot summers. The winds there are moderate, except when the occasional hurricane sweeps up from the West Indies. Collecting during these rare storms is not a good idea, but after a strong wind is over there may be many shells on the beach.

from North Carolina to Texas

Rocky shores and cliffs are unusual in this area, so you will not find limpets and periwinkles here. You will, however, find rock pools. There is no better protected area for some types of mollusks than the pool of clear sea water left by the receding tide, where there are no rough waves to contend with.

Common Jingle
(Anomia simplex)

This jingle is commonly found attached to logs or dead shells from Cape Cod to Texas. It has a strong, smooth, thin shell with an irregular oval shape. The upper valve is convex. The lower valve is flat with a large hole near the hinge. This jingle's shell is a translucent orange or yellow with a silvery-sheen, but when buried in mud, the shell turns black.
Jingle shell family
About 1½ in (4 cm) long

Humphrey Wentletrap
(Epitonium humphreysii)

The Humphrey wentletrap has a slender, thick shell, which is dull white. It has 9 or 10 convex whorls, each with 8 or 9 ribs. The outer lip of the aperture is rounded and thickened. This wentletrap is common on sandy shores from Cape Cod to Texas.
Wentletrap family
About ¾ in (2 cm) long

Brown-band Wentletrap
(Epitonium rupicola)

This wentletrap can be distinguished by its moderately stout whitish to yellowish shell, which is marked with two broad brown bands on each whorl. A few shells of this species are dark brown. There are 12 to 18 ribs on each whorl. This mollusk is common from Cape Cod to Florida and Texas.
Wentletrap family
About ½ in (1 cm) long

Angulate Wentletrap

(Epitonium angulatum)

Wentletraps are sea snails with tall, spiral-shaped shells. The odd name comes from a Dutch word for a winding, or spiral, staircase. The moderately stout shell of the angulate wentletrap is pure white. It has 8 whorls with 9 or 10 thin ribs. This snail is very common and may be found buried in the sand near the sea anemones on which it feeds. Its range is from New York to Texas.

Wentletrap family
About 1 in (2.5 cm) long

Four-toothed Nerite

(Nerita versicolor)

The shell of this nerite has a white, gaping mouth with four strong teeth. Its shell is a dirty-white with squarish black and red marks. It is found clinging to intertidal (see pg. 22) rocks from southern Florida to Texas.

Nerite family
About ¾ in (2 cm) long

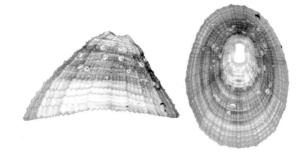

Cayenne Keyhole Limpet

(Diodora cayenensis)

Like other keyhole limpets, the cayenne keyhole limpet has a keyhole-shaped opening near the apex of its single shell. This shell has many irregular radial ribs, every third or fourth being larger than the rest. The outside of the shell typically has white, grayish, and brownish coloring, while the inside is often pale gray. This limpet is very common on rocks from New Jersey to Florida.

Keyhole limpet family
About ¾ in (2 cm) long

Bleeding Tooth

(Nerita peloronta)

The bleeding tooth gets its name from its aperture, which has white teeth on a light red background. It has a solid, sturdy shell. Like other members of its family, it is a sea snail of tropical waters. It is commonly found clinging to intertidal rocks along the southeast coast of Florida. It may also be found above the high tidemark.

Nerite family
About 1 in (2.5 cm) long

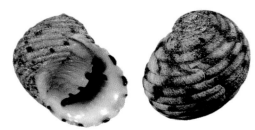

Chestnut Latirus
(Leucozonia nassa)

Its color, a rich chestnut-brown, gives this spindle its name. The light colored aperture has fine white threads. The shell is stubbier than that of many other spindles, with 9 large nodules on the shoulder of each whorl. This animal is common on rocks at low tide from Florida to Texas.
Latirus family
About 1½ in (4 cm) long

American Horse Mussel
(Modiolus americanus)

This mussel clings to rocks and broken shells. It is an offshore bivalve, but it is sometimes washed ashore after a storm. It is common on beaches from North Carolina to Florida and Texas. The shell is light brown with pale purple rays. It has a brown, sometimes hairy, overlayer. The inside of the shell is white, stained with blue, brown, or rose. It is sometimes called a tulip mussel.
Mussel family
About 2 in (5 cm) long

Turkey Wing
(Arca zebra)

The turkey wing is a type of clam that has filelike teeth along the hinge. Its shell is much longer than it is deep and has brown and white zebralike stripes. It flourishes attached to rocks, often covered with other marine growth. You may find it washed ashore after a storm. It is common from North Carolina to Texas. It is also known as the zebra ark.
Ark clam family
About 3 in (7.5 cm) long

Scaly Scallop
(Caribachlamys sentis)

This small scallop lives attached to the underside of rocks in the intertidal zone (see pg. 22). Its valves are nearly flat and have about 50 ribs. One ear is prominent, the other is very small. The shell's bright colors vary greatly. It is common from North Carolina to southeast Florida and the West Indies.
Scallop family
About 1 in (2.5 cm) long

Atlantic Kitten Paw
(Plicatula gibbosa)

The high, rounded ribs and wavy margin of this small scallop give it its popular name. The shell is thick. The hinge has two strong pegs in the upper valve, which fit into sockets in the lower valve. The species is common and is found attached to rocks and shells in the intertidal zone from North Carolina southward.
Kitten paw family—About 1 in (2.5 cm) long

Transverse Ark
(Anadara transversa)

The left valve of the transverse ark overlaps the smaller right valve. The shell is covered with a grayish-brown overlayer. The shell has 30 to 35 ribs, usually beaded on the left valve, but rarely beaded on the right valve. The species is common in sandy mud below the low tidemark from Massachusetts to Texas.
Ark family—About 1 in (2.5 cm) long

Zebra Periwinkle
(Nodilittorina ziczac)

This little periwinkle has a gray shell. There are 20 to 26 fine, reddish, wavy lines on each whorl, like the stripes on a zebra. The species is common in rock crevices on the shores of southeastern Florida. It is also called a zigzag periwinkle.
Periwinkle family
About ½ in (1 cm) long

Sand & Mud Flats

from North Carolina to Texas

Sand and mud flats (nearly level tidal areas) provide homes for many species of mollusks. These areas are uncovered only at low tide—don't confuse them with sandy beaches that slope into the water. Collecting in these flats can be very good, especially by following trails in the sand, or by digging below clam holes.

A snail that lives in these habitats will use its large foot to creep across the sand. Many snails feed on fragments of edible material—animal and vegetable—that are found on the surface. Some bivalves burrow into the sand or mud, leaving just their feeding siphons projecting. Many of these bivalves are filter feeders, drawing in water and filtering out edible particles from it.

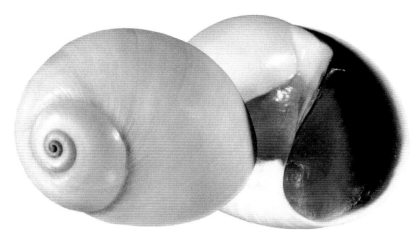

Shark Eye
(Neverita duplicata)

The shark eye is named for its appearance, owing to the buttonlike, brown callus on its otherwise glossy, light tan or gray, globular shell. It is one of a family known as moon snails, which eat clams. It is common on sand flats from Massachusetts to Texas. Its egg mass is coated with sand and formed into an open dome.
Moon snail family
About 2½ in. (6.5 cm) long

White Baby Ear
(Sinum perspectivum)

The white baby ear is also a moon snail. It has a flat white shell covered with fine spiral lines. The animal, which completely fills the shell's large aperture when alive, feeds on small bivalves. It commonly burrows in the sandy beaches of the southeastern United States.
Moon snail family
About 1½ in (4 cm) long

Checkered Nerite
(Nerita tessellata)

The checkered nerite gets its name from the small black dots on its dirty-white shell. This nerite is common in intertidal rock pools from Florida to Texas. It is also called a tessellate nerite.

Nerite family
About ½ in (1 cm) long

Blood Ark
(Anadara ovalis)

Named for the color of the clam that lives inside, the shell of the blood ark is white and has a blackish-brown overlayer that is hairy and fairly thick. The shell has 26 to 35 smooth ribs. The blood ark is common in shallow waters from Cape Cod to Texas.
Ark family
About 2 in (5 cm) long

Ponderous Ark
(Noetia ponderosa)

The ponderous ark, as its name implies, has a solid, heavy shell. The valves are the same size, and their beaks point backward. The 27 to 31 ribs are square, with a fine line down their center. This ark is common in warm waters from Virginia to Texas.
Ark family
About 2 in (5 cm) long

Purplish Tagelus
(Tagelus divisus)

The valves of this razor clam form a broad, flattened cylinder. The shell is fragile and smooth, whitish-purple in color with a very thin, glossy, brown overlayer. This clam is common on sand flats from Cape Cod to Texas and the West Indies.
Razor family
About 1½ in (4 cm) long

Southern Horse Mussel
(Modiolus squamosus)

This mussel is found in muddy or sandy shallow waters. It has a strong, oblong, swollen shell. The outside is brownish-purple with a whitish ray. It is a sub-species of the cold-water northern horse mussel, and it is commonly found off the southeastern United States. It is also called the false tulip shell.
Mussel family
About 2 in (5 cm) long

Sand & Mud Flats

from North Carolina to Texas

Florida Fighting Conch

(Strombus alatus)

Like all members of its family, this conch (pronounced: kahngk) feeds on red algae. The conch moves forward in a series of hops, using its sickle-shaped operculum (or trap-door) as a vaulting pole. Its eyes are on the ends of short stalks. The thick outer lip of the shell flares outward and there are short spines on the spire. This conch genus is common in shallow water from North Carolina to Texas.
Conch family
About 3 in (7.5 cm) long

Atlantic Fig Snail

(Ficus communis)

This sea snail has a long, thin, conical shell, with the aperture running almost the full length of the shell. The shell's spire is very flat. Crisscross lines cover the outer surface. The Atlantic fig snail feeds on sea urchins and related animals. It is found from North Carolina to Texas and Mexico, on sandy beaches where the water is shallow. It is also called a common fig shell.
Fig shell family—About 3 in (7.5 cm) long

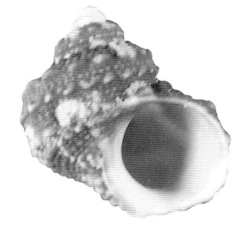

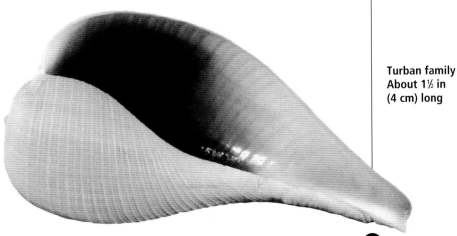

Turban family
About 1½ in (4 cm) long

Chestnut Turban

(Turbo castanea)

Like other turbans, the chestnut turban lives in warm and shallow water feeding on algae. This mollusk has a heavy shell with beading; the shell sometimes has tiny spines as well. It is common offshore in bays from North Carolina south to Texas and the West Indies.

Flamingo Tongue
(Cyphoma gibbosum)

The outside of this stout, glossy shell is cream with orange edges. The aperture runs the length of the shell. In the living creature the mantle extends to cover the shell completely. The mantle is spectacular—it is a light peach in color, speckled with orange dots rimmed in black. The snail is common on sea fans (a type of coral) in shallow water from North Carolina to the islands of the West Indies.
Ovulid family
About 1 in (2.5 cm) long

Scotch Bonnet
(Phalium granulatum)

The square spots on the shell of the Scotch bonnet form a pattern that slightly resembles a Scottish tartan, which is how the shell got its name. The whorls have spiral grooves and beaded cords. The Scotch bonnet lives in shallow, tropical waters. The female lays a tower of eggs, on which she perches. The animal's shell is found washed ashore from North Carolina to western Florida. It is the state shell of North Carolina.
Bonnet and helmet shell family
About 3 in (7.5 cm) long

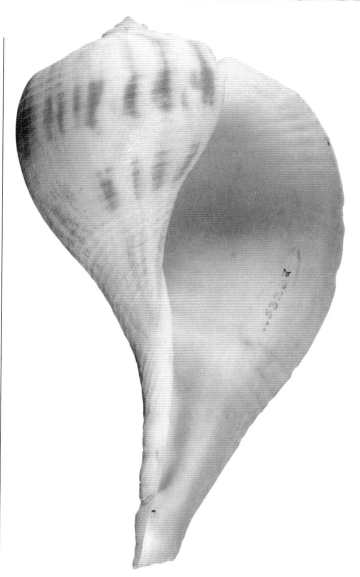

Pear Whelk
(Busycotypus spiratus)

The pear whelk has a shell that usually features smooth, rounded shoulders and is pale with a tan-colored, fuzzy overlayer. This whelk is common from North Carolina to Texas.
Busycon whelk family
About 5 in (12.5 cm) long

Sand & Mud Flats

from North Carolina to Texas

Broad-ribbed Carditid
(Carditamera floridana)

This little clam has a heavy, solid shell, with 15 to 20 raised, beaded radial ribs. The overlayer of the shell is gray. It is very common in shallow water from southern Florida to Texas and Mexico.
Cardita clam family—About 1 in (2.5 cm) long

Florida Cone
(Conus anabathrum)

The Florida cone's range is from North Carolina around to the western coast of Florida. It is another colorful shell and comes in a variety of shades, often white with bands or patches of orange or yellow. Like all cones, it has tiny teeth on its radula (a tonguelike organ). It uses these teeth to inject poison into its prey. This cone is common on sandy flats.
Cone shell family—About 1 in (2.5 cm) long

Florida Prickly Cockle
(Trachycardium egmontianum)

The prickly cockle is named for its 27 to 31 prominent prickly ribs. The two valves are well-domed and elongated from the bead end. The shell's color is white with brownish markings, with bright pink and purple markings inside. It is found from North Carolina to Florida.
Cockle family—About 2½ in (6.5 cm) long

West Indian Dove Snail
(Columbella mercatoria)

This tiny snail is usually colored white and brown. Its shell is squat and heavy and has a thick outer lip. This snail is common in shallow water; it is often found on the seaweeds on which it feeds. Its range is from southeastern Florida to the West Indies. It is also known as the common dove shell.
Dove snail family—About ¼ in (0.5 cm) long

Eastern Auger
(Terebra dislocata)

This auger, which is also called the Atlantic auger, is long and narrow. The whorls on its shell are separated by a lighter spiral band. The shell's color is light gray, banded with reddish-brown and grayish-purple. This auger can be found from Virginia to Texas and makes it home on the sandy bottom in shallow water. Augers have a poisonous tooth and are carnivorous.
Auger shell family
About 1½ in (4 cm) long

Apple Murex
(Chicoreus pomum)

Its strong, spiny shell is the clue to identifying the apple murex, a predator of bivalves and a scavenger of freshly dead sea animals. The spines of this murex are not very long. The shell features yellow, tan, or orange near the inner lip of the aperture, while the outer lip has brown spots. The apple murex is common in shallow waters in the southeastern United States.
Murex family
About 2½ in (6.5 cm) long

Purplish Semele
(Semele purpurascens)

You need to go to tropical waters to find the most colorful semele clam shells, but some, like the purplish semele, can be found elsewhere in the sand or mud. The colors of the purplish semele shell are bright and vary from purple to orange, while the inside is glossy, and purple, brown, or orange. The shell is thin, but strong, with fine growth lines. It is common from North Carolina to Texas and south to South America.
Semele clam family—About 1¼ in (3 cm) long

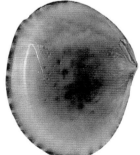

Collecting Expedition

For your expedition, you need the right clothing and equipment. It doesn't really matter what you wear, as long as it suits the weather. Remember that the sun at the beach can be very strong, and you can easily be sunburned. Use sunscreen and choose protective clothing. Read the Collector's Code (page 2) before you start.

What you wear on your feet is especially important. On soft sand and mud it's fun to go barefoot, but a lot of litter can be washed on to beaches, including sharp objects such as cans, broken glass, and jagged pieces of plastic. On rocky beaches, the rocks themselves can cause cuts, so always wear boots or shoes.

Be sure to have a companion with you when you go out collecting, and tell a responsible adult where you will be.

Where to look

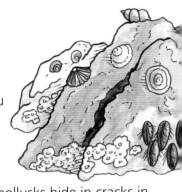

You can find live limpets and periwinkles clinging to rocks at the shore. You may also find barnacles and mussels there, and the saltwater snails that prey on them, such as whelks.

Some mollusks hide in cracks in the rocks. If, however, a mollusk has burrowed into the rock by drilling a hole, then it is probably a piddock (see pages 74-77). Piddocks and the destructive ship-worms sometimes bore into wood. Examine pieces of driftwood to see if you can find them.

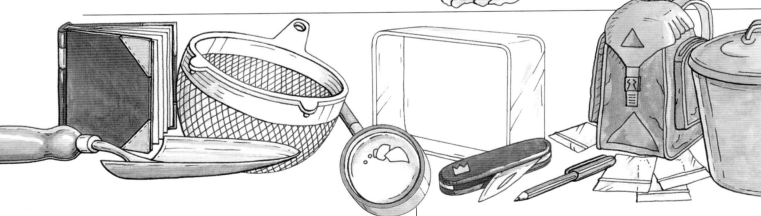

Equipment

The following equipment is useful for finding specimens, examining and recording them, and taking them home. However, it always is best to leave live specimens where you find them. This is particularly true of endangered species.

1 **A spade or trowel:** is essential to dig up live burrowing mollusks from sand and mud.
2 **A kitchen strainer:** to strain out very small shells from sand or mud.
3 **A clear plastic box:** to inspect pools.
4 **A good magnifying glass:** to examine specimens closely. Buy one with a magnification of 10X.
5 **A field notebook:** to keep a record of what you find and where (see opposite).
6 **A waterproof pen.**
7 **A plastic bucket.** One with a tight lid is best, for transporting live specimens. Fill it with seawater.
8 **Small plastic bags:** for empty shells.
9 **A light backpack:** to carry everything in.

Jetties, posts, and piers on sand beaches are also worth checking for piddocks and mussels.

If you pick up a live mollusk to examine it, you should put it back where you found it when you are done. If you want to take it home, turn to pages 50-51, which explain how to care for live mollusks.

Live bivalves are generally hiding in burrows in the sand or mud.

You will need your spade or trowel to dig them out. It is not an easy task, and razor shells in particular are more skilled at hiding than you will be at finding them. You are just as unlikely to uncover marine worms. It will pay you to sieve the sand or mud as you dig, because so many mollusks are tiny. Be prepared to turn over rocks and look beneath them. Some marine snails live on seaweeds that could be growing on the underside of rocks at the beach. On windy days, press the clear plastic box onto the surface of the water in rock pools. You'll be able to see the occupants without disturbing them. You can often find a rich haul of mollusks which have been exposed by the receding tide. Check under the overhang of the rocks and lift up seaweeds, as well.

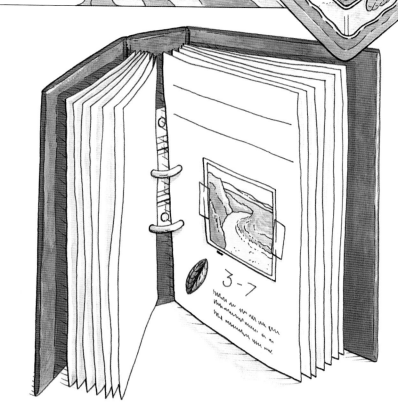

Keeping a record

Your field notebook is essential for recording how and where you found a shell, and interesting information about the beach and the nearby area at the time you made your find.

1 **When you go to a new beach,** give it a special number and make a note of the date and what sort of habitats it has (rock pools, sand flats, etc). Perhaps you can take a photo for your record file?

2 **Each time you visit** that beach, record where the tide was and what the weather was like.

3 **When you find a mollusk or an empty shell,** make a note of the habitat in which you found it, whether any other mollusks were around, and what other animals or features were nearby.

4 **Write the beach's special number** on the outside of each bag, add the date, and number the bag. Use the same number in your notebook that you assigned to the bag, so that later you can match up your notes to the correct shell.

Estuaries & Salt Marshes

from North Carolina to Texas

An estuary is where a river meets with a sea or ocean. The waters of river estuaries are brackish—that is, they contain a mixture of salt water from the sea and fresh water from the river. Brackish water is also found in salt marshes—shallow bodies of water close to the sea. Only certain species of mussels and clams do well in brackish water, and some types of oysters enjoy this habitat. Wading birds, ducks, and crabs feed on estuary mollusks.

Lunar Dove Snail

(Astyris lunata)

In spite of its tiny size, this snail is an aggressive carnivore. It belongs to a family most of whose members live in tropical waters. The lunar dove snail has a smooth, translucent, glossy shell, gray with brown or yellow stripes. It is a very common shallow-water species, especially in weedy areas of estuaries from Massachusetts south to Texas and the West Indies.

Dove snail family
About ¼ in (0.5 cm) long

Hooked Mussel

(Ischadium recurvum)

This small mussel is named for its distinctive shape. The shell is flattish and wide, with many axial ribs. The outside of the shell is a dark grayish-brown, while the inside is purplish to rosy-brown, with a narrow blue-grey border. The mussel is common, often found on wood-piling structures, in brackish water from Cape Cod to Texas and the West Indies.

Mussel family
About 1½ in (4 cm) long

Pointed Nut Clam
(Nuculana acuta)

This is a tiny clam whose shell is rounded at the front end and pointed at the rear. The shell has concentric threads, evenly sized and evenly spaced, and it is white, with a thin, yellow overlayer. This clam is common in the sandy mud lying beneath shallow water from Cape Cod to Texas and the West Indies.
Nut clam family
About ¼ in (0.5 cm) long

Convex Slipper Snail
(Crepidula convexa)

The aperture of this little slipper shell is almost perfectly oval-shaped. Most of the shells of this species are highly arched and dark brown in color with a reddish to purplish tinge. Some specimens may be spotted. Some shells are thick and heavy, but those found attached to other shells are fragile. Slipper snails that settle on eelgrass grow long, narrow shells. The range of this slipper snail is from Massachusetts to Texas and the West Indies.
Slipper snail family
About ½ in (1 cm) long

Yellow Egg Cockle
(Laevicardium mortoni)

This cockle has a thin, yet strong, shell that is small, swollen, and oval. The shell has a smooth, glossy texture and predominantly yellowish coloring. The yellow egg cockle is a common food for ducks. This cockle's range is from Cape Cod to Texas. It is also called the Morton egg cockle.
Cockle family
About 1 in (2.5 cm) long

Elongate Macoma
(Macoma tenta)

This small tellin clam has a fragile shell shaped like an elongated oval. The hinged end of the shell is slightly twisted to the left. The outside is white, with a delicate iridescence. Inside, the shell is a glossy white tinged with yellow. The species is common from Cape Cod south to Florida and the West Indies.
Tellin family
About ¾ in (2 cm) long

Estuaries & Salt Marshes

from North Carolina to Texas

The southeastern coasts of the United States are particularly rich in estuaries and salt marshes. They are home to those mollusks that thrive in a habitat of brackish water and warm climate. In Florida and the Gulf of Mexico, mangrove trees typically grow at the edge of these areas.

Common Atlantic Marginella
(Prunum apicinum)

Like other margin snails, this one is able to move over the shallow sea bottom very quickly, despite its small size. The spire of the shell is stubby; it is very glossy and golden or orange-brown in color. In the Florida Keys you may find a gray variety, however. They are very common in sandy-bottomed shallow areas from North Carolina to Texas and the West Indies.

Margin shell family—About ¼ in (0.5 cm) long

Striate Bubble
(Bulla striata)

There are several species of these snails. Some produce shells that are strong, others that are fragile; some shells are cylindrical, others bulbous. This species has a smooth, white shell with brownish markings. Like other bubble snails, this snail is a hermaphrodite (each animal has both male and female sex organs). It is common on grassy mud flats from North Carolina to southeastern Florida. It is also known as the West Indian bubble.

Bubble shell family
About ¾ in (2 cm) long

Stout Tagelus
(Tagelus plebeius)

The stout tagelus lives in the sand that lies beneath shallow water. It has an oblong, almost cylindrical shell that never completely closes. The exterior of the shell is smooth, with tiny, irregular scratches. The overlayer is brownish-yellow, while the inside is whitish. It is moderately common from Cape Cod south to Texas.

Sanguin clam family
About 3 in (7.5 cm) long

Longspine Star Snail
(Astralium phoebium)

Like other turban snails, the longspine star snail has a heavy shell. This snail is found in southeastern Florida, hiding in grassy shallows. It can be identified by its many spines and the generally low spire. Seen from above, the shell looks like a many-rayed star, which is how it got its name.

Turban family
About 1½ in (4 cm) long

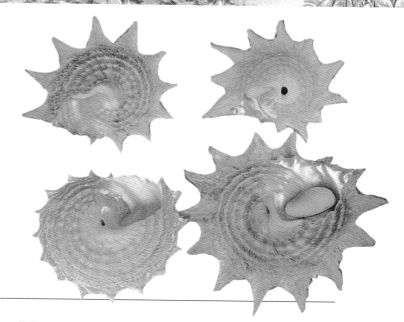

Mangrove Periwinkle
(Littoraria angulifera)

This periwinkle is one of a group of similar species living in the Gulf of Mexico and Caribbean Sea. It has a thin, strong shell, which is nearly smooth, with many fine spiral lines. The color of the shell varies, but the aperture is whitish. This species is common from southern Florida to Texas and the West Indies; it is often found on the branches of mangrove trees. It is also called the angulate periwinkle.

Periwinkle family—About 1 in (2.5 cm) long

Carolina Marsh Clam
(Polymesoda caroliniana)

The Carolina marsh clam is commonly found in river estuaries from Virginia to northern Florida, and also in Texas. It has a strong, bulbous shell, usually worn away at the beaks of the valves. The overlayer is a glossy brown and is covered with tiny, shining scales.

Marsh clam family
About 1¼ in (3 cm) long

Pacific Coast: Alaska to Central California

The Pacific Coast of the United States and Canada supports its own types of mollusks. As on the Atlantic Coast in the east, the terrain and climate of this coast varies considerably. Alaska and British Columbia, the northernmost part of the continent, have a long coastline on the Pacific with hundreds of bays, fiords, and other inlets, many of them rocky.

While the climate is generally cold, southern Alaska and western Canada are warmed by the North Pacific Current and the winds that blow over that ocean current. Glaciers and rivers flow into these waters from the bleak Alaskan mountain regions. The area is called the Aleutian province.

The coastlines of southern British Columbia, Washington, and Oregon are generally rugged, with many miles of cliffs close to the shore and with rocky beaches. Sandy beaches are found between high headlands and there are many river estuaries. The Oregonian province extends south to central California.

The waters of the Pacific Ocean in this region vary from cool to cold. Not surprisingly, the area is dominated by rock-dwelling species of sea snails, cold-water whelks, and Arctic clams. Edible shellfish—like clams, oysters, and scallops—are common in this region.

Rocky Shores & Pools

from Alaska to Central California

At high tide, rocky shores can have waves so rough that they wash most living organisms away. But at low tide you may find limpets and periwinkles clinging to rocks, or sometimes under hanging seaweed. There is no better protected area for some types of mollusks and other sea creatures than the pools of clear water that are left by the receding tide, where there are no rough waves to contend with. The northern Pacific coast of North America is one of the best places in the world to hunt for shells, especially limpets.

All limpets live on rocks. Each limpet's shell grows to fit the patch of rock where it spends its time, so that when it settles down, not even the strongest wave can dislodge it. Often the rim of the shell wears into the rock slightly, giving an even better fit. Limpets may move around at night or at high tide in order to graze on algae, but they return in the morning to their home patch.

Fenestrate Limpet
(Tectura fenestrata)

The fenestrate limpet lives among loose boulders set in sand. It feeds only at high tide. The shell is almost round and is high and smooth. As far south as Oregon the shell is a plain, dark gray, but Californian species are gray-green with cream spots. The inside shell has a brown spot at the center. This limpet is common from Alaska south to California.
American limpet family
About 1¼ in (3 cm) long

File Limpet
(Lottia limatula)

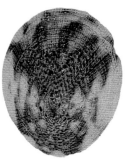

This limpet has a low apex, and its shell varies in shape from elliptical to almost circular. The shell is covered with rows of beads forming tiny radial ribs. The shell's outside is greenish-black, while inside it is a glossy white tinged with blue. The inner shell often has patches of brown with a solid band of brown near the edge. It is common from Puget Sound in Washington down to southern California.
American limpet family
About 1¼ in (3 cm) long

Seaweed Limpet
(Discurria insessa)

As its name suggests, the seaweed limpet is found on large kelps (a type of large, brown seaweed). This limpet has a small, solid shell, with a high spire. The shell is twice as long as it is wide and is a uniform, greasy-looking light brown. A similar-looking species, the black limpet, is black inside and out and clings to several kinds of large snails. Both limpets are very common from Alaska to the peninsula of Baja California in Mexico.
American limpet family
About ½ in (1 cm) long

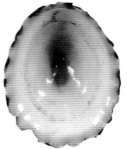
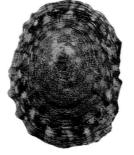

Mask Limpet
(Tectura persona)

This limpet is common from Alaska to northern California. It lives in rock crevices that are formed by the action of the waves. It feeds mostly during low tides at night. The shell is a longish oval in shape, with a fairly high apex pointing forward about one-third of the way from the front edge. The shell's outside is dark gray with a fine pattern of white and brown spots. Inside, the shell is bluish-white to blackish-blue in color.
American limpet family—About 1¼ in (3 cm) long

Pacific Plate Limpet
(Tectura scutum)

From Alaska to Oregon, this limpet is common on rocky shores, but it is rare further south. It has a flat, smooth, almost circular shell with the apex near the center. The shell's outside is greenish-gray and mottled or banded in slate-gray. The inside is pale blue, with alternating bands of dark brown and blue-gray around the rim.
American limpet family—About 1½ in (4 cm) long

Shield Limpet
(Lottia pelta)

This limpet is common in the intertidal zone (see p.22) from Alaska to Mexico. It has a strong elliptical shell with a high apex near the center. The shell has about 25 faint ribs and features a slightly wavy edge. The outside is creamy-gray, with strong black stripes. The inside is mostly a pale blue to white.
American limpet family—About 1 in (2.5 cm) long

Rough Keyhole Limpet
(Diodora aspera)

The outside of this limpet's shell is covered with rough radial ribs, which is how this limpet got its name. The "keyhole" is almost round, and it is located slightly toward the front. The outside of the shell is gray-white with purple-blue radial bands. The inside is blue-white. This limpet is commonly found on rocks from the low tidemark downward or on the stalks of kelp. It is found from Cook's Inlet, Alaska, to southern California.
Keyhole limpet family—About 1½ in (4 cm) long

Dark Dwarf-Turban
(Homalopoma luridum)

This is one of the few turban snails to live in cold water, most of the rest of the family being tropical. The dark dwarf-turban is frequently washed ashore from Alaska to Baja California, Mexico. It has a small, solid, globular shell, varying in color from pinkish- to brownish-red. The last whorl and the base have between 15 and 20 evenly sized, smooth spiral cords. This snail is also known as a carpenter dwarf-turban.

Turban snail family
About ½ in (1 cm) long

Little Margarite
(Margarites pupillus)

Trochoid snail family
About ½ in (1 cm) long

The shell of this snail is shaped like a top. The shell has five or six whorls with many spiral cords. The color of the shell varies from chalky-white to yellowish-gray. The aperture is rosy or greenish. The snail is common from Alaska to Oregon, but it may also be found as far south as San Diego, California. It is also called a puppet margarite.

Blue Top Snail
(Calliostoma ligatum)

This snail has a solid and heavy shell with well-rounded whorls. The shell's background color is chocolate brown covered with smooth, light brown cords. Occasional specimens have a mauve tinge. The aperture of the shell is pearly-white. This snail lives among stones and algae and is commonly found from Alaska to northern California, but it is rare farther south. It is also known as the western ribbed top shell.

Trochoid snail family
About ¾ in (2 cm) long

Black Tegula
(Tegula funebralis)

The head and tentacles of this snail are completely black. In males the sole of the foot is usually a light cream, while that of females is brown. The heavy, solid shell is dark purple-black and is usually smooth. The snail is a very common rock-dwelling species from Vancouver, British Columbia, to Baja California, Mexico.

Trochoid snail family
About 1½ in (4 cm) long

Variegate Amphissa
(Amphissa versicolor)

This little snail is common in the intertidal zone (see p. 22) from British Columbia to the peninsula of Baja California in Mexico. Although small, it is an aggressive carnivore. It has an elongated shell, which is thin but strong, with 7 glossy whorls. The whorls have about 15 slanting axial ribs. The color is pinkish-gray, mottled with orange-brown. It is popularly known as Joseph's coat amphissa.
Dove snail family
About ½ in (1 cm) long

Lurid Dwarf Triton
(Urosalpinx lurida)

The lurid dwarf triton is carnivorous, like all snails of the rock shell family. The species is most common in intertidal areas from southern Alaska to northern California. The shell is shaped like a top, with an elongated spire, rounded whorls, and many rough spiral cords. The color varies from off-white to a rusty-brown. The overlayer is fuzzy and dark brown.
Murex family
About 1 in (2.5 cm) long

Checkered Periwinkle
(Littorina scutulata)

This small marine snail has a longish shell with a pointed spire. The shell is smooth and almost glossy and ranges in color from light to dark reddish-brown. The shell often has irregular bluish or white spots, giving it a checkered appearance. This species is common in the upper intertidal zone from Kodiak Island, Alaska, to California.
Periwinkle family
About ½ in (1 cm) long

Oregon Triton
(Fusitriton oregonensis)

Most tritons are large and live in warm waters, but the Oregon Triton is common in the cold waters near the shore from Alaska to British Columbia. The species is found in deeper water south to southern California. The shell is spindle-shaped and covered with a thick, fuzzy, heavy overlayer of grayish-brown. The aperture is white. All tritons are carnivorous.
Triton family
About 4 in (10 cm) long

Rocky Shores & Pools

from Alaska to Central California

Frilled Dogwinkle

(Nucella lamellosa)

The size, shape, and color of the shell of this rock-dwelling snail vary considerably. Some specimens have a smooth outline, while in others the whorls are clearly stepped. The shell may be white, gray, cream, orange, or brown. The snail is very common on rocks from the Bering Strait down to central California.

Dogwinkle family
About 2½ in (6.5 cm) long

File Dogwinkle

(Nucella lima)

This is a common cold-water species found in the intertidal zone (see p. 22). It ranges from Japan through Alaska down to northern California. Its shell is roughly spindle-shaped with a low spire, and the body whorl has between 17 and 20 spiral cords. The outer shell is off-white or orange-brown.

Dogwinkle family
About 1¼ in (3 cm) long

Emarginate Dogwinkle

(Nucella emarginata)

This shell is found in many variations: the spire is usually low, while the color varies from rusty-brown to a dirty gray. The aperture is light brown, and the whorls are covered with coarse spiral cords. This is a very common rock-dwelling species of snail, ranging from Alaska to Mexico.

Dogwinkle family
About 1 in (2.5 cm) long

Dire Whelk

(Lirabuccinum dirum)

A spindle-shaped brown shell encloses this snail. The shell has 9 to 11 low, axial ribs on the body whorl, and a sharp spire. The aperture is a little over half the length of the shell and colored tan. The outer lip of the aperture has many short teeth inside. This species is common in tide pools ranging from Alaska to southern California.

Buccinum whelk family
About 1 in (2.5 cm) long

You are most likely to find these mollusks trapped in rock pools. They are chitons—they look something like a cross between a tortoise and a pill bug. When dislodged from the rock where it lives, a chiton can curl up as a pill bug does.

Chitons have a shell formed of eight hard, overlapping pieces called valves, bound together by leathery flesh called the girdle. A chiton's flat foot occupies most of its underside; its small head has a mouth with a radula, a strip of flesh that holds hard teeth, but no tentacles. Instead of eyes, a chiton has sensory cells, called aesthetes, which detect light. Most chitons are herbivores.

Merten Chiton
(Lepidozona mertensii)

The Merten chiton is oval in shape. The shell color varies, but it is commonly yellow with dark red streaks. Ribs and ridges on the plates give them an appearance like a net. The girdle has alternating yellow and red bands. This chiton is very common in shallow water on rocks from the Aleutian Islands, Alaska, to the peninsula of Baja California in Mexico.

Chiton class
About 1½ in (4 cm) long

Northern Red Chiton
(Tonicella rubra)

The plates of this chiton are rounded in shape. The shell color is light tan with orange-red marbling, and the girdle is reddish-brown. This species is common on rocks at depths of 10-660 feet (3-200 meters). It is found from the Bering Strait to northern California on the Pacific, as well as from Greenland to Connecticut on the Atlantic coast.

Chiton class
About 1 in (2.5 cm) long

Lined Red Chiton
(Tonicella lineata)

The plates of this chiton are smooth and shiny. Their color is orange to deep red, with oblique black lines bordered with white. The shells are white inside. The girdle is bare. This chiton is common in shallow water from Alaska south to California.
Chiton class
About 1¼ in (3 cm) long

Mossy Mopalia
(Mopalia muscosa)

The stiff hairs on the girdle, looking like a fringe of moss, give this chiton its name. Its shape varies from oblong to oval. The shell color can be a dull brown, blackish-olive, or gray. This is a common intertidal species (see p. 22), which ranges along the entire Pacific Coast from Alaska to the peninsula of Baja California in Mexico.
Chiton class
About 1½ in (4 cm) long

Studying Live Mollusks

It is best to leave live specimens where you find them, thereby disturbing them as little as possible. If you take live specimens home to study, however, you must have a suitable place to keep them. Never keep them away from their natural habitat for more than a week.

The shorter the time you keep these animals the better—it is difficult to arrange a suitable supply of food for a mollusk unless you know exactly what it eats. If in doubt, ask a more experienced collector—or check reliable reference sources at a library.

You can observe sea snails in large glass jars, and you may prefer to keep predatory animals, such as whelks, on their own in this way. You can feed them mussels or small clams. Thawed frozen shrimps are also enjoyed by carnivores. Don't feed them more than once or twice a week and remove the food that is not eaten soon after the feeding.

A seawater aquarium

The best place to keep specimens is in a regular aquarium tank. You can buy one in a pet store that specializes in fish tanks. Such a tank should be large enough to allow for a good layer of sand or gravel on the bottom—a 10-gallon (38-liter) tank is large enough.

Concentrate on specimens of species that all require a similar environment. When you want to study something that needs a different habitat you should clean out the tank and start again.

The dealer who sells you the tank may be able to advise you on what else you need. Such equipment may include a filter (although this may remove the small algae that bivalves eat), and an air pump to ensure that the water has enough oxygen in it. (Sea animals absorb oxygen from the water, just as you do from the air you breathe.)

Because you are studying saltwater specimens, you will need to have enough saltwater to fill the tank. Ask an adult to take a supply home for you by car, in a watertight container.

Mark the water level on the side of the aquarium and when it goes down, you can add some rain or pond water to raise the level back to the line. Put a sheet of glass or plastic over the tank to stop the water from evaporating as quickly, but leave a crack for air to circulate.

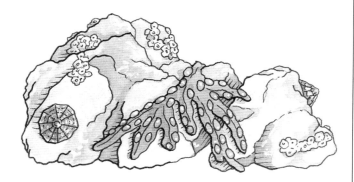

Decorating your aquarium

Try to create a realistic environment for your mollusks. Rocks with algae on them, which you have gathered from the seaside, will appeal to many sea snails—such as periwinkles—and provide food. Some seaweed will help the appearance of the tank and also helps to provide a balanced environment.

Aquariums always function best with a layer of clean pea-gravel at the bottom. But if you want to study a mollusk that lives in mud or sand, you will have to add a solid layer of sand in at least part of the tank for them to burrow into. This sand layer should be 1–2 inches (2.5–5 centimeters) deep.

The water in a saltwater aquarium should be as near as possible to the temperature of the sea that the specimen inhabits. Bear this in mind when deciding where to put your aquarium. For example, it wouldn't be a good idea to put it on a window sill in direct sunlight, as the water would get very warm. Still, remember that in winter, the sea, even near the shore, can be warmer than freshwater ponds or rivers.

Things you might see

The eye of a gastropod peeping out of its shell (this is a pink conch).

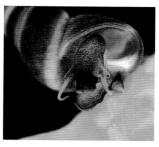

The common northern chink snail on the move with its foot extended.

A cockle with its siphons exposed. This means that it is drawing in water to gather oxygen and food.

A pair of slipper snails mating— they are connected at the top right.

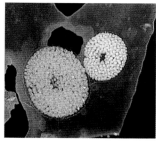

Egg clusters of the common northern chink snail.

Sand & Mud Flats

from Alaska to Central California

Although much of the northern Pacific coast of North America is rocky, there also are long stretches of sand and mud flats between the many rocky headlands. Sand and mud flats (nearly level tidal areas) provide homes for many species of mollusks. These areas are only uncovered at low tide—don't confuse them with sandy beaches that slope into the water. Look for mollusks by following their trails in the sand, or digging below clam holes.

A snail that lives in these habitats will use its large foot to creep across the sand. Many snails feed on fragments of edible material—both animal and vegetable—that are found on the surface. Some bivalves burrow into the sand or mud, leaving just their feeding siphons projecting. Many of these bivalves are filter feeders, drawing in water and filtering out edible particles from it.

Wroblewski's Wentletrap
(Opalia wroblewskii)

Like other wentletraps, this snail is white and its shell is grayish-white, though sometimes it is stained purple by the animal's own dye. The shell is long, solid, and always looks worn. It has six to eight low, wide, axial ribs. This species is fairly common in shallow water from Alaska to southern California.

Wentletrap family
About 1 in
(2.5 cm) long

Beatic Dwarf Olive
(Olivella baetica)

Most olive shells are tropical—this is one of the few species that flourishes in cold water. It is a carnivorous scavenger. Its shell is long with a pronounced peak. The shell color is a glossy tan, with purplish-brown spots. The species is moderately common in shallow water over sand. Its range is from Kodiak Island, Alaska, to the peninsula of Baja California in Mexico.

Olive shell family
About ½ in
(1 cm) long

Wampum Tusk Shell
(Antalis pretiosum)

Wampum is a North American Indian word for beads made from shells. The beads were used to decorate objects. The shell is moderately curved and solid, an ivory-white color, usually with faint yellowish growth rings. It is a common offshore species living in sandy mud from Alaska to the peninsula of Baja California in Mexico.

Tusk shell family
About 2 in
(5 cm) long

Blister Glassy-bubble
(Haminoea esicula)

The shell of this little snail is very fragile. It is globular and a translucent yellow in color, with a thin rusty-brown or yellowish-orange overlayer. It is a common species and can be found in intertidal bays from southern Alaska to Mexico. It is also known as the Gould glassy-bubble.

Bubble shell family
About ¾ in (2 cm) long

Lewis Moon Snail
(Euspira lewisii)

This is a very common clam-eating species, found in shallow water from British Columbia to southern California. It has a heavy, globular shell with a small, brown buttonlike callus at the base.
Moon snail family—About 4 in (10 cm) long

Nuttall Cockle
(Clinocardium nuttallii)

This species is large for a cockle. It has a roundish oval shell with 33 to 37 coarse radial ribs. The ribs carry beads shaped like half-moons, but the shells of older cockles are often worn smooth. The shell color is a drab gray, with a thin, brown-yellow overlayer. This is a common sand-loving cockle, found from the Bering Sea and Alaska to southern California.
Cockle family—About 4 in (10 cm) long

Sickle Jackknife Clam
(Solen sicarius)

This edible clam is identified by its long, rectangular shell, which is very slightly curved. It is covered with an olive-green, varnishlike overlayer. The clam is common on sand and mud flats from British Columbia to California. It is also called the blunt jackknife clam.
Razor clam family
About 3 in
(7.5 cm) long

Pacific Razor Clam
(Siliqua patula)

The shell of this razor clam is oblong and oval-shaped. It is thin, but strong. The olive-green overlayer looks like a varnish. The inside of the shell is glossy and white, tinged with purple. This edible clam is very common from Alaska to central California.
Razor clam family
About 5 in (12.5 cm) long

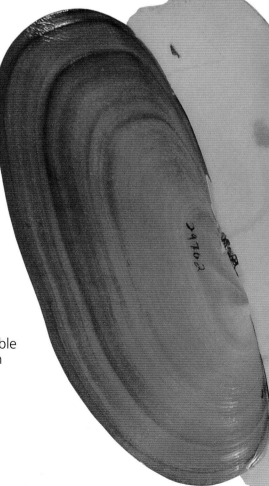

Sand & Mud Flats

from Alaska to Central California

Hooked Surf Clam
(Simomactra falcata)

The low beaks of this clam are near the round back end. The front end is elongated and narrow. The outside of the shell is chalky, with a shiny brown overlayer. Like other surf clam shells, an aid to identification is the spoon-shaped recess in the hinge. This clam is common from Washington to California.
Surf clam family—About 2½ in (6.5 cm) long

Washington Clam
(Saxidomus gigantea)

People in Alaska often eat this venus clam. It has solid, heavy valves, with coarse concentric threads. The valves gape a little at the back end. The shell color is gray-white. This clam is found from Alaska south to northern California.
Venus clam family—About 3 in (7.5 cm) long

California Sunset Clam
(Gari californica)

This clam belongs to a family similar to the tellins (see pgs. 66-67). The main difference between the two is that sanguin clams are bigger. The shell is an elongated oval, with the low beaks nearer the front end. The outside is covered with strong, irregular growth lines. The color is dirty-white with faint purple rays. The overlayer is brown. It is often washed ashore after storms from the Aleutian Islands, Alaska, as far south as California.
Sanguin clam family—About 4 in (10 cm) long

Pacific Littleneck
(Protothaca staminea)

This edible venus clam has a solid shell, sculptured with many concentric and radial ribs. The color of the outside varies from light gray to rusty-brown to dark chocolate-brown. Sometimes the shell has a mottled pattern. The clam is commonly found in shallow water from the Aleutian Islands, Alaska, to the peninsula of Baja California in Mexico.
Venus clam family—About 2 in (5 cm) long

California Softshell Clam
(Cryptomya californica)

Softshell clams are a popular food item. This clam is small, with a fragile, oval shell. The outside is chalky-white with a gray overlayer. The valves gape very slightly at the rear end. It is common in sandy habitats from Alaska to southern California.

**Softshell clam family
About 1¼ in
(3 cm) long**

Macoma
(Macoma yoldiformis)

The Latin name of this tellin comes from Count Yoldi of Denmark, for whom a family of nut clams was named. This tellin has a similar shape to the family known as yoldia nut clams. This macoma is an elongated oval, white in color, and glossy like porcelain. It is common on sand flats from Alaska to California.

**Tellin family
About ½ in
(1 cm) long**

Geoduck
(Panopea abrupta)

In the Pacific northwest, people call this huge, edible clam the "gooeyduck." It is commercially fished in Washington and Oregon. The misshapen shell gapes at both ends. The outside of the shell is dirty-white to cream in color, with a thin, yellowish overlayer. The inside is white and somewhat glossy. The geoduck lives in mud at the bottom of a burrow some 2-3 feet (0.6–0.9 meters) deep. It is found from Alaska to Mexico.
**Saxicave clam family
About 8 in (20 cm) long**

Alaska Great-Tellin
(Tellina lutea)

This tellin's strong shell is a large elongated oval, the shell color is chalky-white, commonly flushed with pink, while the overlayer varies from green to brown. This species is commonly found in the intertidal zone and at depths to 130 feet (40 meters) from Japan to Alaska and British Columbia.
**Tellin family
About 4 in (10 cm) long**

Your Shell Collection

Mollusks produce large numbers of young to ensure their species' survival, since such a large number of predators hunt them. This makes it unlikely that one collector could affect the survival rate of any species. Still, it is better to collect and study only the shells. Be sure to find out if collecting in your chosen area is legal. Some states have laws against collecting shells, whether the animals inside are alive or not.

Cleaning

When you take your shells home, the first thing to do is to clean them. Most empty shells only need to be rinsed in clean cold water, and perhaps brushed over with an old toothbrush. Be very careful with more fragile shells. If there is a crust or scale on a shell, you can scrape and chip it away, but try not to remove any of the natural coating or weathering of the shell.

If you want to preserve the shell of a specimen that has died recently, you will have to remove its soft parts. To do this, put the shell in a saucepan of cold water, bring the water to a boil and leave it boiling for about 10 minutes. Leave the water to cool naturally, or you may damage the shell.

Or you can put the shell inside a plastic box or bag and place it in the freezer. After 1 to 2 days, remove it and let it thaw. The soft parts will then easily slip away from the shell. **Always ask permission before you use the stove, saucepan, or freezer.**

BLUE MUSSEL
Cockle Bay 3-6

9-9
WINKLE

Labeling

When you have cleaned your shells, put them in trays (like the trays that supermarkets use to package vegetables) or plastic boxes, and label each one. Very small shells can be kept in glass or plastic tubes, plugged with cotton.

Your label should give the popular name of the specimen, the scientific name if you know it, when and where you collected it, and any other important or interesting information.

Equipment

This is the equipment you need to manage your collection, along with your field notebook and magnifying glass (see page 36):

1 **An old toothbrush** for cleaning specimens.
2 **A penknife** for cutting away the animal's soft parts.
3 **A dental tool** to scrape away encrustations.
4 **A sharp point** for cleaning small holes. You can make one by inserting the blunt end of an old darning needle into a cork.
5 **Tweezers** for picking up and holding tiny shells.
6 **Cotton swabs** for cleaning out shells.
7 **A short ruler** for checking the size of a shell.
Be careful when using sharp tools.

A home for your collection

It's very easy to make some simple storage units to hold the shells in your collection. They shouldn't cost very much and you can add to them at any time.

All you need are some shoe boxes (with their lids) and some stiff paper. Then what you do is:

1 **Measure the shoe box** across its short side and its depth. Draw a rectangle **(A)** on the stiff paper to match this size (for instance, 5 X 6 in, or 12 X 15 cm). Draw two lines across the rectangle to divide it into three sections.

2 **Measure the long side** (for instance, 5 X 12 in, or 12 X 30 cm) Draw another rectangle **(B)** to match this size. Draw two lines across it to divide it into three.

3 **Cut out each rectangle;** then cut another one each of **(B)** and **(A),** using your first rectangles as your patterns.

4 **Line the bottom of the box** with thin foam padding if you like. Then cut halfway up each dividing line of each partition and slot the partitions together as shown. Last, slide the partitions into the box.

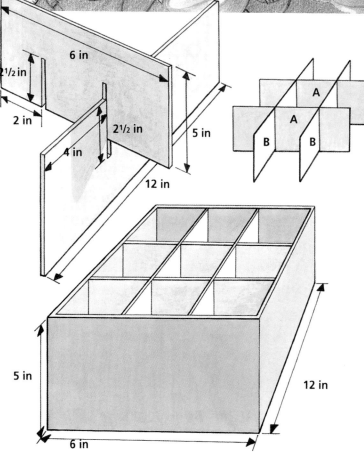

5 **Paint the boxes and their lids** with latex paint so that they all match. Keep shells of the same family together, and write their name or draw a picture of them on the short end of the box.

Small scale storage

You can use aluminum foil or plastic cling wrap boxes to store small shells.

1 **Measure the end of the box** (for instance 2 X 2 in, or 5 X 5 cm) and draw a strip of these squares on some stiff paper (card).

2 **Cut out a strip** and bend it into a series of right angles as shown at left.

3 **Fit the bent card into the box** and glue the sides to the box. Paint these boxes to match your large storage boxes, if you like.

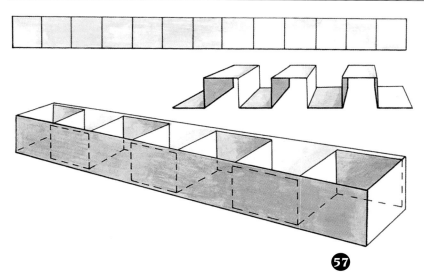

Pacific Coast: Southern California

California extends over more than half the length of the Pacific Coast of the continental United States. Most of California—from Point Conception south—makes up what malacologists (zoologists who study mollusks) call the Californian province.

Southern California, from around Santa Barbara southward, has many wide, sandy beaches. The state's rivers provide estuaries where species of mollusks that are suited to brackish water can breed and flourish.

California's climate is mild, particularly in the south, where it can be very hot in the summer. (Surface sea temperatures are about 75 °Fahrenheit [24 °Celsius].) Mollusks that prefer warmer water flourish here.

Rocky Shores & Pools

of Southern California

At high tide, rocky shores can have waves so rough that they wash most living organisms away. But at low tide you may find limpets and periwinkles clinging to rocks, sometimes under hanging seaweed. There is no better protected area for some types of mollusks and other sea creatures than the pools of clear seawater that are left by the receding tide, where there are no rough waves to contend with. The southern Pacific coast is not as rich in rock-dwelling mollusks as is the northern Pacific area, but a few rock-dwelling mollusks, such as limpets, may be found in the south.

All limpets live on rocks. Each limpet's shell grows to fit the patch of rock where it spends its time, so that when it settles down, not even the strongest wave can dislodge it. Often the rim of the shell wears into the rock slightly, giving an even better fit. Limpets may move around at night or at high tide in order to graze on algae, but they return in the morning to their home patch.

Two-spot Keyhole Limpet

(Fissurellidea bimaculata)

Both the shell and the large "keyhole" of this limpet are in the shape of an elongated oblong. Many radial and concentric threads give a crisscross appearance to the shell. The outside of the shell is brownish to gray in color. The inside is glossy white. The animal is several times larger than its shell. This limpet is common under stones from the low tidemark downward.
Keyhole limpet family
About ¾ in (2 cm) long

Eroded Periwinkle

(Littorina keenae)

A typically badly worn section of the shell gives this periwinkle its name. The shell is small with a pointed spire. The shell color is gray-white with bluish-white spots. The aperture is chocolate-brown with a white spiral band at the bottom. This snail is very common on rocky flats in the splash zone (see pg. 22), from Puget Sound in Washington state to Baja California in Mexico.
Periwinkle family
About ¾ in (2 cm) long

Volcano Keyhole Limpet

(Fissurella volcano)

The volcano limpet is a typical keyhole limpet, and it does look like a miniature volcano. It has a fairly high, oval-shaped shell, with an oblong "keyhole" that looks like the volcano's crater. The shell has many large, low radial ribs. The outside is gray, with pinkish-mauve radial rays, while the inside is glossy white. In California this limpet is common on rocky rubble in the intertidal zone.
Keyhole limpet family
About 1 in (2.5 cm) long

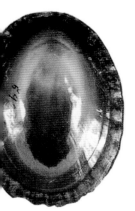

Owl Limpet
(Lottia gigantea)

This is indeed a giant among limpets, it is commonly found on rocks at the tidemark from California to Mexico. The apex of its massive shell is near the front end. The brown, rough, and sometimes algae-covered shell is glossy inside, with a wide brown border and a bluish central area, sometimes stained brown.
Limpet family—About 4 in (10 cm) long

Rough Limpet
(Lottia scabra)

The name of this limpet comes from its wavy edge, which is produced by its 15 to 20 strong, coarse, radiating ribs. The shell is a dirty gray-green on the outside and white with a brown stain on the center of the inside. It is common from Oregon to the peninsula of Baja California in Mexico. You may find this limpet clinging to gently sloping rock surfaces high above the water line within reach of the ocean spray.
American limpet family
About 1 in (2.5 cm) long

Scaled Worm Snail
(Serpulorbis squamiger)

These snails live in colonies attached to rocks or wharves, just below the low-water mark. Their home is a tubelike shell, which is gray or pinkish. This snail cannot leave its shell and feeds by trapping particles in the water using thin, sticky, mucus threads. This species is common from California to as far south as Peru.
Worm snail family
Tube diameter about ½ in (1 cm)

Giant Keyhole Limpet
(Megathura crenulata)

This is one of the largest American keyhole limpets. It is found from central California to the peninsula of Baja California in Mexico. Because this limpet is good to eat, it is becoming scarce in Mexico. The animal is black, and its mantle fills up most of the shell. The outside of the shell is mauve to brown, covered with fine beads. The "keyhole" has white edges.
Keyhole limpet family
Between 3–6 in
(7.5–15 cm) long

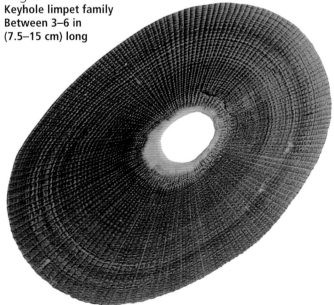

Poulson Dwarf Triton

(Roperia poulsoni)

The shell of this species is solid with a semiglossy finish. Each whorl has eight or nine lumpy ribs, crossed by many, very finely cut spiral lines. The grayish or brownish overlayer is thin and smooth. This is a very common species on rocks and wharves, particularly in the southern part of its range—which is from California to Mexico.
Murex family
About 1½ in (4 cm) long

Checkered Unicorn

(Acanthina paucilirata)

This snail's solid shell has six spiral rows of small, black-brown squares on a cream background that give the shell a checkerboard appearance. The outer lip of the aperture also has brown squares, and there is a small, needlelike spine at the base of the aperture. This snail is common on rocks above the mid-tidemark from California to Mexico.
Murex family
About ½ in (1 cm) long

Spotted Unicorn

(Acanthina punctulata)

Small, red-brown spots on a blue-gray shell give this snail its name. (A variety that is completely yellow is sometimes found.) The shell is low-spired, solid, and smooth except for numerous, faint spiral threads. This snail is common at the high tidemark along rocky shores and among the beds of the mussels on which it feeds. The spotted unicorn is found from Puget Sound in Washington state to southern California.
Murex family
About 1¼ in (3 cm) long

Livid Macron

(Macron lividus)

The strong, solid shell of this whelk is somewhat yellow in color and covered with a thick, feltlike, dark brown overlayer. The shell has five whorls. There are six spiral lines cut at the base of the shell. This little whelk is very common and can be found under stones and in rock pools at low tide. Its range is from California south to Mexico.
Buccinum whelk family
About 1 in (2.5 cm) long

Kellet Whelk
(Kelletia kelleti)

A very heavy, solid shell is made by this large snail. The bottom of each whorl has 10 strong, rounded knobs, and the base of the shell has 6 to 10 cut spiral lines. The aperture is glossy and white. This snail is very common from northern California to Mexico in rocky areas below the high tidemark. People use baited traps to catch this edible whelk.
Buccinum whelk family
About 4 in (10 cm) long

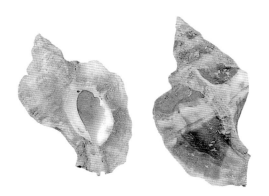

Nuttall Thorn Purpura
(Ceratostoma nuttalli)

Like other murex, this species produces a small quantity of purple dye. It has a solid, heavily knobbed, yellow-brown shell, which sometimes features spiral bands. The animal has a long, sharp spine on the outer lip (the thorn), which it uses to open barnacles. It is common in the southern part of its range—from California to Mexico.
Murex family
About 1½ in (4 cm) long

Secret Jewelbox
(Chama arcana)

This sturdy, spiny bivalve is commonly found attached to wharves, wood pilings, and jetties. It is found from Oregon south to Mexico. The white shell is occasionally tinged with pink or olive. The shell has broad, translucent frills, and the hinge has a large, irregular tooth. It is also called the clear jewelbox.
Jewelbox family
About 2 in (5 cm) long

Sand & Mud Flats

of Southern California

Sand and mud flats (nearly level tidal areas) provide homes for many species of mollusks. These areas are uncovered only at low tide—don't confuse them with sandy beaches that slope into the water. Look for mollusks by following trails in the sand, or digging below clam holes. Although much of the northern Pacific coast of America is rocky, there are also extensive stretches of sand and mud flats between the many rocky headlands.

   A snail that lives in these habitats will use its large foot to creep across the sand. Many snails feed on fragments of edible material—both animal and vegetable—that are on the surface. Some bivalves burrow into the sand or mud, leaving just their feeding siphons projecting. Many of these animals are filter feeders, drawing in water and filtering out edible particles from it.

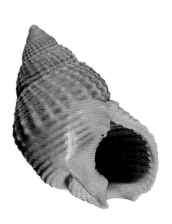

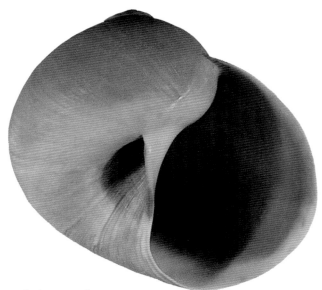

Channeled Nassa
(Nassarius fossatus)

The channeled nassa is the largest species in its family. Its shell is orange-brown to gray; the last whorl has about 12 coarse, spiral threads crossed by short axial riblets. It is common in intertidal zones (see pg. 22) from Vancouver Island in British Columbia to Mexico. It is also known as the giant western nassa.
Nassa mud snail family
About 1½ in (4 cm) long

Oldroyd Moon Snail
(Calinaticina oldroydii)

A thin, globular shell that is a little wider than it is high distinguishes this snail. There is an umbilicus (hole) in the base of the shell. This snail lives in large colonies offshore, in sandy areas from Oregon to southern California. There it feeds on small bivalves and lays its eggs in open domes of sand.
Moon snail family
About 2½ in (6.5 cm) long

Green Glassy-bubble
(Haminoea virescens)

A very large, open aperture and a fragile shell are characteristics of this little snail. The translucent globular shell is green-yellow in color. The animal is dark green with yellowish markings. This snail is a common, shallow-water species of the open coast. It prefers sandy areas where there are beds of sea grass. There it lays its egg masses on weed stems. It is found from Puget Sound in Washington state to Baja California in Mexico.
Bubble shell family
About ½ in (1 cm) long

Purple Dwarf Olive
(Olivella biplicata)

The purple dwarf olive has a solid, glossy shell. The shell color can range from brownish to bluish-gray, and there are violet stains around the lower part of the aperture. During the summer months this snail is very common in sandy bays and beaches. It ranges from Vancouver Island in British Columbia to the peninsula of Baja California in Mexico.
Olive shell family
About 1 in (2.5 cm) long

Carinate Dove Snail
(Alia carinata)

The shoulder of the last whorl of this tiny shell is swollen, forming the "carina"—a ridge shaped like the keel of a ship—which gives the species its name. The shell is smooth and glossy; its color is a mixture of orange, white, and brown. This is a common shallow-water species, which is found on weeds in sandy areas from California to Mexico.
Dove snail family
About ¼ in (0.5 cm) long

Fat Western Nassa
(Nassarius perpinguis)

Neat, beaded sculpturing characterizes the shell of this nassa mud snail. Its shell is thin, but strong, with a straight, pointed spire. The aperture is less than half the length of the shell. Most of the shell is yellow-brown. This species is extremely common on intertidal flats (see pg. 22) off Vancouver Island in British Columbia, south to Baja California in Mexico.
Nassa mud snail family
About 1 in (2.5 cm) long

Sand & Mud Flats

of Southern California

Californian Surf Clam

(Mactrotoma californica)

This is a small clam, fairly common in lagoons in the California region. Its smooth shell is in the shape of an elongated oval and is somewhat fragile. There are concentric undulations on the shell's beaks. The overlayer is a velvety yellow-brown. There is a small, spoon-shaped hollow in the center of the hinge.
Surf clam family
About 1½ in (4 cm) long

Senhouse Mussel

(Musculista senhousia)

This small mussel was introduced from Asia and now flourishes from Washington to California. It makes its nest on mud flats and clings to wooden pilings. The smooth shell is small, thin, and fragile. It is green to blue-green in color with brown zigzag marks.
Mussel family
About 1 in (2.5 cm) long

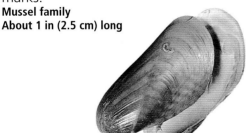

Plain Tellin

(Tellina modesta)

Commonly found in sandy areas from Alaska to Mexico, the plain tellin is a small, thin-shelled bivalve. The shell is long and somewhat pointed at the hinge. It has fine concentric threads and is white with an iridescent (rainbowlike) sheen. The two hinge teeth are very small.

Tellin family
About ¾ in
(2 cm) long

Fat Horse Mussel

(Modiolus capax)

This common mussel can be found along the Pacific coast from California to Peru. It lives in huge colonies below the high tidemark. It has a strong, swollen shell that is oblong in shape. The shells are orange-brown in color, with a thick, hairy overlayer. (The specimen in this photo has lost its overlayer.)
Mussel family—About 4 in (10 cm) long

Salmon Tellin
(Tellina nuculoides)

Smaller than the plain tellin, the salmon tellin has a white, oval shell with several widely spaced growth lines that are stained dark brown. The inside of the shell is a salmon-pink color. It is common from the low tidemark and below, and it ranges from the Aleutian Islands in Alaska to southern California.
Tellin family
About ½ in (1 cm) long

California Mussel
(Mytilus californianus)

This mussel has a large, thick shell. The shell's lower edge, opposite the hinge, is curved. The outer surface has coarse growth lines and about 12 weak radial ribs. It is very common in the intertidal zone (see pg. 22) from the Aleutian Islands in Alaska to Mexico.

Mussel family
About 5 in (12.5 cm) long

Pacific Gaper
(Tresus nuttalli)

The Pacific gaper is a very large clam with an elongated, oval shape. It gapes open at the rear end. This common species lives in sandy mud in shallow water from California to Baja California in Mexico.
Surf clam family
About 8 in (20 cm) long

Sand & Mud Flats

of Southern California

Bent-nose Macoma

(Macoma nasuta)

The rear end of the shell is compressed and strongly twisted to the right—hence its common name. The shell is sturdy and chalky-white. The left valve is nearly flat. There are two tiny teeth at the center of the narrow hinge. It is a very common species, living in mud in quiet waters from southern Alaska to Baja California in Mexico.

Tellin family
About 3 in (7.5 cm) long

White-sand Macoma

(Macoma secta)

This fairly large, white bivalve lives in sand in bays and intertidal flats and is common from British Columbia to Mexico. The glossy white shell has an almost flat left valve and an inflated right valve. There is a large, riblike ridge behind the hinge inside each valve.

Tellin family—About 3½ in (9 cm) long

California Butterclam

(Saxidomus nuttalli)

This clam is only found between northern California and the peninsula of Baja California in Mexico. In this range it is a very common, edible species, living in shallow water. The shell is solid and oblong. The outside of the shell is covered with coarse, crowded, concentric ribs. The shell color is a dull reddish-brown, varying to gray. The inside is a glossy white with touches of purple.

Venus clam family—About 3½ in (9 cm) long

California Lyonsia
(Lyonsia californica)

The small, elongated shell of this clam is very fragile—it is almost transparent. The shell's outside is opalescent white and is commonly covered with the weak, darker radial lines of the overlayer. The species is common in California in the sandy mud bottoms of marshy inlets and bays.
Lyonsia clam family
About 1 in (2.5 cm) long

Japanese Littleneck
(Venerupis philippinarum)

This clam was introduced, probably accidentally, from Japan and it now flourishes in the waters of Puget Sound in Washington state and off the coast of California. Its shell is almost egg-shaped, and the beaks are nearer the front end. The shell's outside has radial threads and is beaded at the hind end. The inside of the shell is tinged with purple.
Venus clam family
About 2 in (5 cm) long

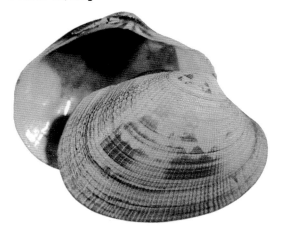

Pismo Clam
(Tivela stultorum)

From California to Mexico, this edible clam is a common shore species. It has a large, heavy shell, which is glossy and smooth except for weak growth-lines. The shell color is brownish-cream with wide, mauve-colored radial rays. The overlayer is thin and glossy.
Venus clam family
About 4 in (10 cm) long

Punctate Pandora
(Pandora punctata)

The punctate pandora is a small, flat, cold-water clam that lives in sandy mud from the low tidemark and down to 120 feet (36.5 meters) deep. The shell is crescent-shaped. The species is common from Vancouver Island in British Columbia to the peninsula of Baja California in Mexico.
Pandora clam family—About 1 in (2.5 cm) long

Estuaries & Salt Marshes

of Southern California

An estuary is where a river meets with a sea or ocean. The waters of estuaries are brackish—that is, they contain a mixture of salt water from the sea and fresh water from the river. Brackish water is also found in salt marshes. These are shallow bodies of water close to the sea. Only certain species of mussels and clams do well in brackish water, and some types of oysters also enjoy this habitat. Wading birds, ducks, horseshoe crabs, and blue crabs feed on estuary mollusks.

California Bubble
(Bulla gouldiana)

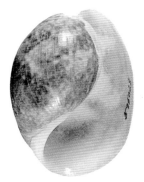

The shell is large for a bubble, and the animal is even bigger than the shell. The aperture extends the full length of the shell, which is a grayish-brown with darker brown streaks. The snail is most active at night, but also look for it on mud flats at low tide.
Bubble shell family
About 1½ in (4 cm) long

California Venus
(Chione californiensis)

This sturdy shell has many low, radial ribs that are crossed by raised concentric ribs, giving it a checkerboard appearance. The inside of the shell is white with a purple blotch at one end. It is found from southern California to Panama. This edible clam lives in sand from the intertidal zone (see pg. 22) to areas below.
Venus clam family
About 2 in (5 cm) long

Pacific Littleneck
(Protothaca staminea)

This clam is valued as a food item; fortunately, it is very common in the intertidal zone. The species is found from Alaska to the peninsula of Baja California in Mexico. The shell has many radial and concentric ribs. The shell on the outside varies in color from light gray to rusty-brown to dark chocolate-brown.
Venus clam family—About 2 in (5 cm) long

California Bean Clam
(Donax californicus)

This wedge clam has a thin shell that is longer and slightly larger than that of its relative, Gould's donax. The shell's outside is yellowish-white, with a tan or greenish overlayer. Inside it is off-white with a purple blotch at each end of the hinge. This species is common in the intertidal zone from California to Baja California in Mexico. Look for it in coves and bays.

Wedge clam family
About 1 in
(2.5 cm) long

Norris Snail
(Norrisia norrisi)

This top snail lives among kelp (large, brown seaweed), eating the food particles that cling to the seaweed. It is common from Monterey, California, to the peninsula of Baja California in Mexico. The shell is smooth, heavy, and solid. It is a glossy, blackish-brown. The operculum is circular and has rows of dense bristles.
Top snail family
About 1½ in (4 cm) long

Northern Lacuna
(Lacuna vincta)

This tiny lacuna periwinkle is a cold-water species, and it is common offshore in shallow water. It is found living on kelp. It ranges from Alaska to California on the Pacific Coast, and from Newfoundland and Labrador south to Rhode Island on the Atlantic Coast. It has a fairly thin, but strong, translucent shell. There is a small chink, or slit, in the bottom of the shell; the shell's outside is smooth except for microscopic spiral scratches. Color varies from light tan to brown, with the spire tinted a purplish-rose. It is sometimes called a chink shell.
Lacuna periwinkle family
About ¼ in (0.5 cm) long

San Diego Date Mussel
(Adula diegensis)

This little mussel has a shape typical of the family, elongated and slightly curved. It is also called a non-boring date mussel to distinguish it from most other date mussels, which bore into rock. This mussel's shell is chestnut-brown. It is a very common species, living in colonies attached to wharves, pilings, and jetties. It is found from Oregon south to Mexico.

Mussel family
About 1 in
(2.5 cm) long

Green False Jingle
(Pododesmus macrochisma)

The almost circular shell of this species is fairly strong, with very coarse, irregular radiating ribs. The lower valve has a hole. The shell's color is greenish-white and inclined to be pearly. It is commonly found on stones, wharves, and pilings, but it may also be found on other shells, particularly abalone shells. It lives all around the Pacific from Japan across to Alaska and down to Mexico. It is also known as the false Pacific jingle.
Jingle shell family—About 3 in (7.5 cm) long

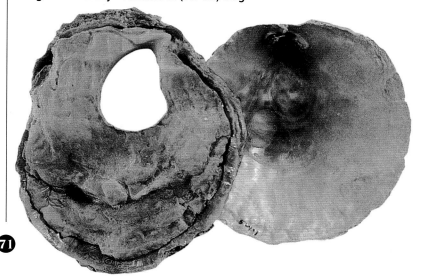

Things to Make

Many shells can be used decoratively. Some of the large tropical shells can be ornaments on their own, but many small shells can be used to decorate other objects.

Decorate with shells

The best way to attach shells to an item is to put a layer of modeling clay or ready-mixed wall filler (spackle) over the object you wish to decorate—a box, vase, or bottle, for instance. Press the shells of different sizes and colors into the clay to make a pattern. After the clay dries, you can coat the object with varnish to protect it and give it a glossy finish.

Wreath of shells

This is a good way of displaying your shells and also makes an unusual present.

1 **Take a generous handful of straw** and twist it into a "snake."
2 **Wind thin wire tightly round** the straw to hold it together and make it tight and firm.
3 **Bring the two ends of your "snake" together** and overlap them. It will help if the ends are thinner than the rest of the "snake." Use the wire to then bind it into a ring.

4 **You can attach shells** to this ring with wire or pins, but it is better to stick them on with white craft glue.

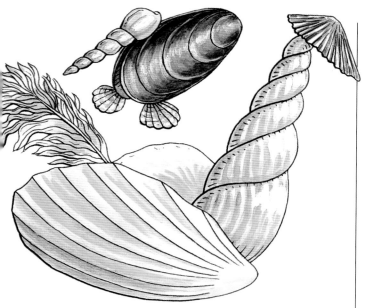

Birds and monsters

Use two different gastropod shells glued together to make a series of "exotic birds." Add a small feather to form the tail and make them more lifelike.

You can also invent your own creatures by sticking together shells to make "monsters." Don't stick more than two shells together at a time, and let those shells then dry before adding more.

Jewelry from the sea

Small shells make beautiful and unusual jewelry. Why not make yourself a pendant or a pin?

1 **Buy a bell cap and ring** from your local craft or hobby store and some white craft glue.
2 **Choose a fine example of a shell.** Wash the shell carefully in warm soapy water and leave it to dry.

3 **Glue the bell cap to the top** of your shell and leave it to dry.
4 **Thread the ring through** the bell cap and pinch the ring tight (you may need help for this). Thread the pendant on to a ribbon or chain.

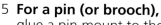

5 **For a pin (or brooch),** glue a pin mount to the side of the shell next to the opening as shown.
6 **To make the shells shine,** you can paint a coat of varnish over them.

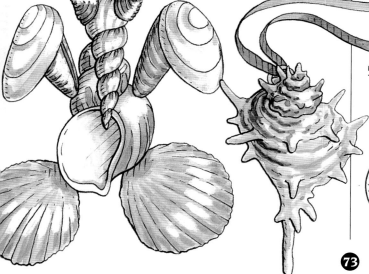

Wood & Rock Borers

of the Atlantic *Coast*

The borers are a group of bivalves which, as might be expected, bore holes. Some borers tunnel into wood and others into rock. The animal bores with the front edge of the shell, which it rocks back and forth to wear away the wood or rock.

Borers are all bivalves, but they come from a diverse range of families. Most of them bore to make a home where they can shelter from predators.

Gould Shipworm
(Bankia gouldi)

These so-called shipworms are not worms at all, though they have long bodies like earthworms. They are bivalves, but with very small shells that enclose no more than a fraction of the animals' bodies. In the days of wooden ships these animals were a menace to vessels they infested. As the picture at left shows, the damage caused by shipworms is immense.

Living animals are common in floating logs, wharves, pilings, and other underwater timbers. As the shipworm grows, it burrows into the wood, leaving behind a long, shell-lined tunnel that is connected to the open sea. The animal grips the inside of the tunnel with its foot, and twists its valves back and forth to wear away the timber. It absorbs food from the seawater, which it takes in through a siphon which protrudes from the open end of the tunnel. It can also digest some of the cellulose from the timber. In all species, the siphons can be withdrawn, and the end is then closed by a pair of feathery, limy plates that are called "pallets."

There are about two dozen species of shipworms; their identification is difficult, and can be made only with live specimens. Gould shipworm is a common shipworm.
Shipworm family
About 8 in (20 cm) long

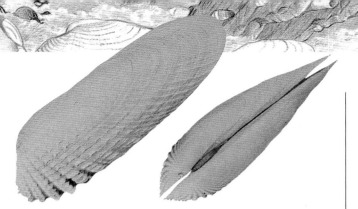

False Angel Wing
(Petricolaria pholadiformis)

You can see from this picture why this shell is called the false angel wing. If you see a live specimen, you will see it has large, translucent, gray siphons. It bores holes into peat and clay and is common from the Gulf of St. Lawrence to Texas. It has a long, fragile, chalky-white shell.
Rock borer family—About 2 in (5 cm) long

Striate Piddock
(Martesia striata)

This little piddock is usually pear-shaped, although the shape varies. The foot-gape between the two valves is wide. The shell is white, with a tan overlayer. This piddock is common in floating or submerged wood from North Carolina to Texas and south to Brazil. The animal can only be extracted from its wooden home with a sharp tool.
Piddock family
About 1 in
(2.5 cm) long

Angel Wing
(Cyrtopleura costata)

The two valves of this huge clam look very much like the wings artists have drawn for angels. The long, thin shell is pure white with a thin gray overlayer. Each valve has about 30 beaded axial ribs. It is common in shallow water, where it burrows almost 12 inches (30 centimeters) deep in the mud. It is found in the southeastern United States in quiet waters.
Piddock family—About 6 in (15 cm) long

Oyster Piddock
(Diplothyra smithii)

This tiny bivalve also belongs to the family of boring clams known as piddocks. It is small, oblong, and wedge-shaped and has a white shell. It tunnels into soft rocks or, as here, into the shells of oysters. It is common from Massachusetts south to Texas.
Piddock family
About ½ in (1 cm) long

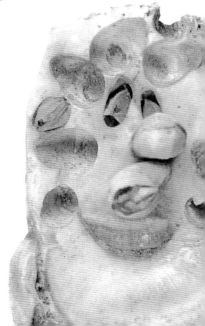

Wood & Rock Borers

of the Pacific Coast

The Pacific coast has a number of piddocks that bore into clay or sand for shelter. Unfortunately, it also has destructive shipworms (see page 74).

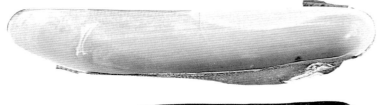

Curved Date Mussel

(Adula gruneri)

This is a fairly common rock-borer in shallow water from Coos Bay, Oregon, to Mexico. It has a very elongated, cylindrical shell, which is slightly curved. The beaks of the valves are about one-eighth the length from the swollen front end. The color is a shiny chestnut-brown.
Mussel family
About 3 in (7.5 cm) long

California Date Mussel

(Adula californiensis)

This is similar to the falcate date mussel, but chubbier and much smaller. It has a smooth surface and is chocolate-brown in color. A velvety, hairy overlayer covers the back end. The mussel makes burrows in hard rocks in shallow water. It is fairly common from British Columbia to southern California.
Mussel family
About 1 in (2.5 cm) long

Straight Horse Mussel

(Modiolus rectus)

This large mussel lives buried in mud. It has a rectangular shell that is slightly curved. Thin growth lines cover the outside, which is bluish-white with a yellowish-brown overlayer. The inside is pearly-white, with a touch of pink. Its range is from British Columbia to Mexico.
Mussel family
About 5 in
(12.5 cm) long

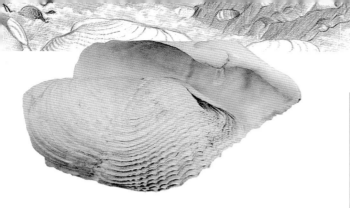

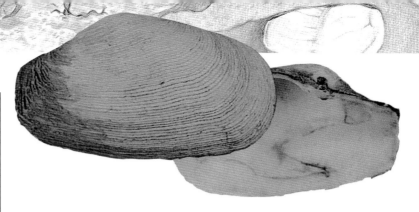

Monterey Piddock
(Penitella richardsoni)

This borer tunnels into sandstone rocks and clay from Alaska to southern California. Its siphons are fused together. The shell is thin, but strong, with an oblique groove across the outside. It is white in color with yellowish marks. It is also known as a Gabb piddock.
Piddock family—About 2 in (5 cm) long

Boring Softshell Clam
(Platydon cancellatus)

This clam lives in holes it bores in hard-packed clay or soft sandstone. It has a solid, oblong shell covered with concentric lines that look like clapboard (the overlapped wooden boards used to side a house). The outside is chalky-white, with a thin overlayer that is brownish or rust-colored. This clam is found from British Columbia to southern California.
Softshell clam family—About 2½ in (6.5 cm) long

Flap-tip Piddock
(Penitella penita)

This is the most common piddock to be found along the Pacific coast. It bores into hard clay, sandstone, and cement, and you can find it from Alaska all the way down to Mexico. Its siphons are smooth, with flaps on the end. The valves of its shell are elongated ovals.
Piddock family—About 3½ in (9 cm) long

Wartneck Piddock
(Chaceia ovoidea)

You will find the burrow of this large piddock in soft shale rock below the low tidemark. This piddock has a fat, oblong shell, divided by an oblique groove in the middle of each valve. The species is found from California to Baja California in Mexico.
Piddock family—About 3 in (7.5 cm) long

Find Out More

Glossary

aperture: main opening of a gastropod shell

apex: point of the spire on a gastropod shell

beak: first part of a bivalve's shells to form, just above the hinge

bivalve: mollusk with two shells, or valves, hinged together, such as a clam or oyster

byssus: threadlike structure used by mollusks to anchor themselves to rocks

canal: channel at the lower end of a gastropod shell through which the siphon is extended

contrary: any gastropod shell coiled to the left

cord, spiral: horizontal band on a whorl

ear: handlelike structure found on scallop shells on each side of the hinge

filter feeder: animal that lives in water and takes in small pieces of drifting material for food

gape: opening between the two valves that remains even when a bivalve is closed

gastropod: mollusk with a single shell, which may be either coiled or cap-shaped, such as a snail or conch

hermaphrodite: animal having both male and female sex organs

hinge: pivoting point from which a bivalve opens and closes

intertidal zone: shore between the points of high tide and low tide

ligament: muscle that holds the two valves of a bivalve together

malacology: study of mollusks

mantle: flaps on a mollusk's body used to attach the animal to its shell

mollusk: soft-bodied animals without backbones; most mollusks, such as snails and clams, have shells.

operculum: hard "trapdoor" that some mollusks have on their feet and use to close themselves inside their shells

overlayer: soft, often hairy layer on the outside of a shell that protects the shell as it grows

pallial line: scar on a bivalve, parallel to the longest side, where the mantle is attached to the shell

radula: ribbon of flesh that bears rows of teeth

ribs, axial: vertical ridges on a whorl

ribs, radial: ridges running from a central point on a shell

sculpture: relief patterns on a shell, such as cords, ribs, knobs, and spines

siphon: tube that mollusks use to take in and expel water and food

spire: all the whorls of a gastropod shell except the lowest one, where the animal lives

tentacle: long, thin, fleshy finger on a mollusk's head for touching things

thread: fine spiral line around a whorl

tooth: shelly ridge in the upper, hinged part of a valve

valve: one of the two shells that make up a bivalve

whorl: one complete turn in a gastropod shell

Organizations

The American Malacological Society is an organization of professionals and hobbyists that publishes the *American Malacological Bulletin.* Write to: The American Malacological Society, 4201 Wilson Blvd., Suite 110-455, Arlington, Virginia 22203-1859. http://erato.acnatsci.org/ams

The **Conchologists of America** is a collector-oriented society promoting shellfish conservation and environmentally sound collecting practices. It publishes the quarterly *American Conchologist.* Write to: Conchologists of America, 1222 Holsworth Lane, Louisville, Kentucky 40222.

For a complete listing of **National Wildlife Refuges,** contact: National Wildlife Refuge System, U.S. Fish & Wildlife Service; (1-800) 344-WILD. http://refuges.fws.gov

For Pacific Coast enthusiasts, there is the **Western Society of Malacologists,** open to professionals and amateurs. Write to: Western Society of Malacologists, P.O. Box 1995, Newport, Oregon 97365. http://biology.fullerton.edu/wsm/index.html

Index

Additional Resources

American Seashells R. Tucker Abbott (Van Nostrand, 1974) and **Seashells of North America** (St. Martin's, 1996).

The Encyclopedia of Shells Kenneth R. Wye (Chartwell, 2000).

Guide to Seashells of the World A. P. H. Oliver (Firefly Books, 2004).

National Audubon Society First Field Guide: Shells Brian Cassie (Scholastic, 2000).

Shells S. Peter Dance (Dorling Kindersley, 2002).

Index